Praise for *Watershed Moments*

Watershed Moments is written with moving prose and packed with amazing testimonies and illustrations of true watershed moments. Gari Meacham undergirds this book with Christ's truths — the true precipitator of any watershed.

—DR. H. EDWIN YOUNG, senior pastor
of Second Baptist Church, Houston, Texas

I have always looked for and embraced life's watershed moments, and Gari Meacham's book *Watershed Moments* has become one for me. Changes in life, no matter if they're planned or unexpected, can be a challenge, but with a friend like Gari by your side, obstacles become opportunities to see God at work. You will like the woman you will become as you read and look for your own watershed moments.

PAM FARREL, author of *Becoming a Brave New Woman* and
Men Are Like Waffles, Women Are Like Spaghetti

In *Watershed Moments*, Gari Meacham writes with the flair of a poetic seamstress, weaving together colorful turns of phrase, bold truth, and healing from a hurtful past to piece together a masterpiece of healing and hope. This book is a joy to read. It will move you to laugh, cry, pray, hug your kids, kiss your spouse, and proclaim, "Our God reigns."

—GARY THOMAS, author of *Sacred Marriage*

Before you open this book, be sure you have a highlighter in your hand. Gari has generously shared precious nuggets she has discovered in countless watershed moments. From the introduction to the last chapter, there are truths you will want to revisit — now get your highlighter ready.

—JACKIE KENDALL, president of Power to Grow, Inc.,
and bestselling author of *Lady in Waiting*

Gari writes with such depth and vulnerability that you feel like you could read *Watershed Moments* for an entire year and find new insight each day. At the same time, you feel like you're having coffee with a lifelong friend and talking through the great and hard moments of life. Her passion to share truth from Scripture and her stark honesty about her own life impact readers in ways that leave them blessed and changed.

—RENÉ TAUBENSEE, director of baseball women's
ministry at Pro Athletes Outreach

Watershed Moments grabbed me from the first page. We've all experienced those moments that opened our eyes to truth and to greater clarity about a particular stronghold or struggle, that prompted us to take a stand or to take a leap of great courage. Gari Meacham zeroes in on those precious moments and squeezes every bit of growth from them. She helps us recognize them as God's personal shout-out to "pay attention." And when we see and listen and obey, God moves, and we are never the same.

—LESLIE VERNICK, counselor, coach, speaker, and author of *Lord,
I Just Want to be Happy* and *The Emotionally Destructive Marriage*

Through rich testimony resting on solid biblical foundations, Gari Meacham reminds us that there are no mundane moments for people in covenant with the Father through Jesus Christ and that God is working amid the dull and shocking times as well as the dazzling and scintillating.

—WALLACE HENLEY SR., associate pastor at Second Baptist Church,
Houston, Texas, and author of *Globequake*

GARI MEACHAM

TURNING POINTS THAT CHANGE
THE COURSE OF OUR LIVES

WATERSHED MOMENTS

ZONDERVAN®

We want to hear from you. Please send your comments about this book to us in care of zreview@zondervan.com. Thank you.

ZONDERVAN

Watershed Moments
Copyright © 2013 by Gari Meacham

This title is also available as a Zondervan ebook. Visit www.zondervan.com/ebooks.

This title is also available in a Zondervan audio edition. Visit www.zondervan.fm.

Requests for information should be addressed to:

Zondervan, *Grand Rapids, Michigan* 49530

Library of Congress Cataloging-in-Publication Data

Meacham, Gari.
      Watershed moments : holy markers that change our lives for good /
Gari Meacham.
           pages   cm
      Includes bibliographical references and index.
      ISBN 978-0-310-30866-9 (softcover : alk. paper)
      1. Life change events — Religious aspects — Christianity. 2. Adjustment
(Psychology) — Religious aspects — Christianity. 3. Change (Psychology) — Religious
aspects — Christianity. 4. Change — Religious aspects — Christianity. I. Title.
BV4509.5.   M375 2013
248.8'6 — dc23   2013012511

Published in association with the Books & Such Literary Agency, 52 Mission Circle, Suite 122, PMB 170, Santa Rosa, CA 95409-5370, www.booksandsuch.com.

Cover design: Curt Diepenhorst
Cover photography: Michael Melford / Getty Images®
Interior design: Katherine Lloyd, The DESK

Printed in the United States of America

13 14 15 16 17 18 /DCI/ 23 22 21 20 19 18 17 16 15 14 13 12 11 10 9 8 7 6 5 4 3 2 1

To the men and women who allowed me
to share their watershed moments —
I'm deeply moved by the clarity and the hope
your turning points have sheltered.

CONTENTS

Acknowledgments

Acknowledgments are the first place I turn to when I look at a book — because I love to see who's behind a writer. I'm fascinated by the people who help an author bring words to a page and meaning from life's pulse. It is with extreme gratitude that I thank those who help me craft meaning from the pulse of my life.

- To Bobby — all our late-night talks and early-morning prayers sustained me throughout this process. You are my compass. Without you I'm adrift.
- To my mom, Joy, my dad, Gary, my sister and brother, Maureen and Sean — I'm forever grateful to have been born into a family that has taught me love and grace with such authenticity.
- To our children, Brooke, Ally, and Colton; and our grandkids, Reese and Roman — your smiles, stories, and passion inspire me to capture life on a page.
- To the women at Second Baptist Church in Houston — every tear, every round of applause, every story you shared inspired me to write about our watersheds.
- To John Sloan and Dirk Buursma — your talent and grace as editors leave me challenged and improved.
- To the entire team at Zondervan — marketing, curriculum, sales, and design — I'm in awe of your tenacity and vision. So thankful to be a part of it.
- Most important, to the cross — the ultimate Watershed, which has left me forever changed.

1

POINTS OF NO RETURN

The night before I gave birth to our third child, I paced back and forth across the blackened pebbles of our driveway. My husband had taken our four- and three-year-old daughters to the unexpected funeral of his mom on the West Coast. With a travel advisory on my late pregnancy, I remained at our temporary home in New Jersey to prepare for our third Cesarean birth. This child was a son, and instead of being excited to view his sweet face the next morning, or feeling anxious that my husband could be delayed in his flight plans and not make it home in time with our two little lambs, I paced the driveway, muttering the same line over and over to a faithful friend who spent the evening comforting me: "Why have I done this to myself again? I know exactly what to expect, and I chose to do this a third time!"

I was lamenting the pain I knew was inevitable — the transition I feared would sling me into chaos. After some early use of my deep breathing techniques meant for labor, I finally whispered, "This is a point of no return. There's no going back. I have to go forward."

What's embarrassing about this point of no return is that I have faced many challenging moments that far surpass childbirth — suffocating moments, perplexing moments, moments that left me begging God to show me his providence.

Our lives are defined by such moments. Some moments pass like the flicker of a winking eye — you barely know they've passed until your eye has closed and reopened, ready for its next blink. Other moments leave you marked — decidedly different from before.

Some moments are laced in glory, joyously happy and giddy in their birth — the moment a man asks a woman to be his bride, the moment you accomplish a goal that seemed impossible, the moment you surrender to God, who beckons you.

Others are tinted with a haze that lifts like fog once we accept their presence — a moment that disappoints, a moment that infuses fear, a moment when we raise our hands in confusion. These are the watershed moments of our lives — the moments God uses to mark us, move us, and alter us for good.

IMPRINT OF A WATERSHED

A watershed moment is a turning point brought on by circumstances that stop us in our tracks. Some call it an epiphany. A moment when everything changes. A point in time when nothing will ever be the same. Like a compass that provides direction, these are the moments that move us to new ways of thinking, relating, discerning, and accepting life's challenges.

In the first part of this book, I share how God uses watershed moments of change, awareness, and restoration to groom us for future glory. Not the kind of glory that spouts praise and accolades for tasks we've accomplished, but glory that wells up when maturity is having its way.

When I was a kid, I loved the thought of becoming mature. Maturity meant I could stay up late, watch different types of shows, eat what I wanted, and push the boundaries of a curfew. But I seldom hear adults begging to mature. We want to stay youthful, free from responsibility, and comfortably detached. The truth is, without moments that sculpt the clay of maturity in our lives, we remain ineffective blobs pleading for purpose. Watershed moments of change, awareness, and restoration shape us so God can lovingly transform us.

Next we'll look at the watershed moments that loosen our need for control and approval. Without these moments, our grip on life is so tight that our knuckles may pop. I have to laugh at the ways I think I manage my life, ways that must provide God with his fair share of entertainment.

I remember hearing a man tell a story that explains this perfectly. In the midst of pain and confusion at his circumstances, he went out to the wooded area behind his house to take a walk. While he strolled under the pine trees, he began to feel a release of tension as he lifted his hands in praise. Suddenly, a small bird landed in his outstretched hands. It literally sat there, peacefully perched in his hands. The man was stunned and instantly shouted to the Lord that this was his miracle — the moment he'd been waiting for when everything murky became clear. Before he finished his sentence, the bird relieved himself all over the man's outstretched hands! At first he was appalled, but then began to laugh as he realized how little control we have over anything — even the moments we think we've figured out.

Finally we'll delve into the watershed moments that empower us to face evil. Evil wears many masks, and as we pull away the scary images that pin us down in fear, we're free to experience a new kind of watershed — the watershed of belief. These are the moments of reckoning in which we march and conquer that which has for too long conquered us.

How can such a word define the essence of the moments that unravel and restore us? How can a watershed moment lead us to the brink of what we've been and create a bridge to what we'll become? I'm both fascinated by this word and inspired by it because God is at the helm of our watersheds, using precise moments to mark momentous transitions and upheavals that take us from one point in our lives to the next.

Even history is defined by the watershed moments that help carve out its destiny. I was surprised by the conclusions of an article called

Top 10 Watershed Moments in History. Here's how the scholars ranked the watershed moments that changed the planet:

#10 The Russian Revolution
#9 Invention of the Watt steam engine
#8 Assassination of Archduke Ferdinand Francis
#7 Black Plague
#6 Storming of the Bastille
#5 Vaccine for smallpox
#4 Invention of the printing press
#3 Protestant Reformation
#2 Berlin Conference
#1 Birth of Jesus of Nazareth

According to this article, the influence Jesus has had on the lives of people throughout history has never been surpassed. Christianity has revolutionized the world, changing how people think and live. No other person has had a greater effect on world history than Jesus Christ.[1]

At first I was impressed with this number one ranking. After being married to a major league baseball player and coach for over thirty years, I love to march around with a big foam finger on my hand and point out, "We're number one!"

But then I whispered two words.

"*Big deal*," I thought. "*Seriously — big deal.*" Who cares if Jesus gets good marks for transforming history if we don't allow him to transform us? In the big picture, it's not going to matter that people respect Jesus; it only matters if they love and accept him. He is the ultimate Watershed, the brilliant turning point that leaves no life the same.

Last night, as I crawled into bed, I wondered how I could write a book on a topic as important as the moments that change us — and my emotions had a field day. It was then that the simple words of my husband, Bobby, penetrated the fog that had settled over me.

"You know what?" he said as he turned over to face me. "To me, watershed moments are the moments we encounter God. We hear from him, sense his presence, or are impacted by a truth he makes known. Don't try to make it more complicated than it is." How I love the simple wisdom of my sports-minded man. God's words, his presence, and his truth change the moments of our lives.

I realize that many of you reading this may sigh like I used to when I wanted to "hear" from God but wasn't sure I ever really had. Let me encourage you, friends — you *will* have your moments. God *will* bring his watersheds. They may come in the form of unexpected blessings or circumstances, but they will come.

Years ago, I read the story of a cab driver (now a highly acclaimed author) who experienced a watershed moment that left him profoundly changed. His watershed didn't come in the form of loud lessons or triumphant victories, but rather in the tender hug of a lonely woman.

There was a time in my life twenty years ago when I was driving a cab for a living. It was a cowboy's life, a gambler's life, a life for someone who wanted no boss ...

What I didn't count on when I took the job was that it was also a ministry. Because I drove the night shift, the car became a rolling confessional. Passengers would climb in, sit behind me in total darkness and anonymity, and tell me of their lives ...

In those hours, I encountered people whose lives amazed me, ennobled me, made me laugh, and made me weep. And none of those lives touched me more than that of a woman I picked up late on a warm August night.

I was responding to a call from a small brick fourplex in a quiet part of town. I assumed I was being sent to pick up some partyers, or someone who had just had a fight with a lover ...

When I arrived at the address, the building was dark except for a single light in a ground-floor window. Under these circumstances, many drivers would just honk once or twice, wait a short minute, and then drive away. Too many bad possibilities awaited a driver who went up to a darkened building at two-thirty in the morning.

But I had seen too many people trapped in a life of poverty who depended on the cab as their only means of transportation. Unless a situation smelled of danger, I always went to the door to try to find a passenger. It might, I reasoned, be someone who needed my assistance ...

So I walked to the door and knocked.

"Just a minute," answered a frail, elderly voice ...

After a long pause, the door opened. A small woman, somewhere in her eighties, stood before me. She was wearing a print dress and a pillbox hat with a veil pinned on it ... By her side was a small nylon suitcase ...

"Would you carry my bag to the car?" she asked ...

I took the suitcase to the cab, then returned to assist the woman. She took my arm, and we walked slowly toward the curb. She kept thanking me for my kindness ...

When we got in the cab, she gave me an address, then asked, "Could you drive through downtown?"

"It's not the shortest way," I answered.

"Oh, I don't mind," she said. "I'm in no hurry. I'm on my way to a hospice."

I looked in the rear-view mirror. Her eyes were glistening.

"I don't have any family left," she continued. "The doctor said I should go there. He says I don't have very long."

I quietly reached over and shut off the meter. "What route would you like me to go?"

For the next two hours we drove through the city. She showed me the building where she had once worked as an elevator operator. We drove through the neighborhood where she and her husband had lived when they had first been married. She made me pull up in front of a furniture warehouse that had once been a ballroom where she had gone dancing as a girl. Sometimes she would have me slow down in front of a particular building or corner and would sit staring into the darkness, saying nothing.

As the first hint of sun was creasing the horizon, she suddenly said, "I'm tired. Let's go now."

We drove in silence to the address she had given me. It was a low building, like a small convalescent home, with a tar driveway that passed under a portico. Two orderlies came out to the cab as soon as we pulled up …

"How much do I owe you?" she asked, reaching into her purse.

"Nothing," I said.

"You have to make a living," she answered.

"There are other passengers," I responded.

Almost without thinking, I bent over and gave her a hug. She held on to me tightly. "You gave an old woman a little moment of joy," she said. "Thank you."

There was nothing more to say. I squeezed her hand once, then walked into the dim morning light. Behind me I could hear the door shut. It was the sound of the closing of a life.

I did not pick up any more passengers that shift. I drove aimlessly, lost in thought. For the remainder of that day, I could hardly talk. What if that woman had gotten a driver who had been angry or abusive or impatient to end his shift? What if I had refused to take the run or had honked once, then driven away …?

We are so conditioned to think that our lives revolve around great moments. But great moments often catch us unawares. When that woman hugged me and said that I had brought her a moment of joy, it was possible to believe that I had been placed on earth for the sole purpose of providing her with that last ride. I do not think that I have done anything in my life that was any more important.[2]

In the dark hours of a routine night, this cab driver experienced a watershed moment — a great moment that caught him unaware, leaving the fragrance of his life entwined with another in a deep pool of hope. A true watershed isn't to be hoarded; rather, it is to be shared, to spread its gift of insight from our life to the lives of those around us. To spill onto another life the clarity that has been spilled onto ours.

MISSING OUR MOMENTS

I hate missing out on things. You know, special events, sales, or gatherings about which people rave and say, "You really should have been there!" I want my senses alert and my spirit sharp so I don't drive by watershed moments in my haste to get somewhere.

What causes us to miss out on life's defining moments? Why do we skip right past those precious seconds that can change us forever? I believe the answer lies in a tangle of *nots*. Often, we're not engaging, not risking, not listening, or not loving. But take heart, because anything we're not doing leaves room for what we can do.

To engage God means we're absorbed with his character and the character of his people. It's hard to be absorbing, however, if you fear getting wet. To engage God means we're engrossed, involved in his living word and purposes here on earth. The essence of a watershed experience is looking at risk and assessing the damage, like this: "I can be safe and ignore my desire for life-changing moments," we might think, "or I can risk comfort and listen for the melody of love to inspire me."

When I first began to explore the word *watershed*, I was with women from my church in Houston. A group of about a thousand women met on Monday nights to try to squeeze the meaning out of the moments that change us. I picked the word *watershed* for our title with very little thought given to its definition, but once we got started, I realized the meaning of this word was painting our gatherings with a color once beige but now dazzling white. Described as a critical turning point — a point from which you can't turn back — I knew we were on to something that would leave its mark long after we finished the study.

In order to remind us to look for our moments, I bought thousands of silver and gold rings from the wedding section of Hobby Lobby. We placed them in plastic champagne glasses and set them around our gathering spot so women could grab them and twirl them on their fingers. The rings were a symbol to cause us to pause and take note of our expectant hope that we'd see God move and that we'd experience our watershed moments.

Many months later, I'm still hearing stories about women's moments and the rings we wore to remind us to look for them, but one young woman's story leaves me breathless.

Lauren shared, "I was raised in a wonderful home with parents who loved each other and loved God. I invited Jesus into my life at an early age, but when I was in elementary school, I was the victim of a sexual assault by a neighborhood friend. At such a tender age I didn't understand what happened and that it wasn't my fault — and by junior high and high school, I was making every bad choice imaginable to numb my pain. If there was a sinful act or addiction I was either doing it or had a friend who was.

"When my eighteenth birthday arrived, I reached a point of bottoming out, and remember lying in my bed, saying, 'God, if you're truly real, let me die. There's no hope for me. I'll always be a disgrace to you.' The next morning, I woke up alive — disappointed and plummeting further into despair.

"During spring break of my senior year, Mom and I took a trip to New York City to celebrate graduation, but once I got there I could barely move I was so sick and overcome with fatigue. Dad met us at a New York City hospital in time to hear a verdict pronounced in the heavy Russian accent of a doctor we barely knew. 'You have leukemia,' he said. We learned that what would normally be a 3 percent leukemia marker in someone's bone marrow was 93 percent in mine.

"My first round of chemo left me in ICU, as my kidneys shut down from the treatment. When I regained consciousness, I opened my eyes and saw a childhood friend, Rebecca, sitting across from me. She had been diagnosed almost a year before with a rare cancer, and there she sat, smiling, with tiny sprays of hair growing into the bald spots left from her treatments. 'Lauren,' she said, 'everything's going to be fine. I'm praying for you, and so are many others.'

"The next months were a blur of complications, leaving me with two

emergency brain surgeries, pneumonia, and pancreatitis, and without
my eyesight—legally blind. Because of my age, I was often treated on
the pediatrics floor, where I got close to many families and their kids.
During the months following my treatment, I attended the funerals of
three beautiful children, as well as that of my precious friend Rebecca.

"I knew I needed to take my brokenness and surrender it to God.
I never dreamed he'd place me in a position of leadership with women,
helping them see his goodness, no matter the circumstance — but after
all I'd been through, I sensed women would listen. Pain is good to
have on your résumé when you teach women about God, because it's
through pain that we become authentic — and I was about as authentic
as you can get.

"Prior to this, I had little time to think about a man, let alone
romance, but soon my heart was awakened to the hope for a relationship with someone I could share my life with. I was introduced to a
man named Clay, but I kept trying to set him up with my best friend
before realizing he was the man *I* hoped for!

"The following spring I was a small group leader for a beautiful
group of women studying watershed moments. Rings were handed out,
and we were told they were to remind us to pray for our moments —
moments that would lead us to never again be the same. I remember
putting mine on and praying, 'Lord, this ring will not leave my finger
until I receive my watershed.' Two weeks after the study ended, the
ring was removed from my finger and replaced with a new one. Clay
asked me to be his wife on March 24, 2012."

These watershed moments that change us aren't predictable or
scripted. They're as fresh as wildflowers and unique as fingerprints,
designed to penetrate the protective layers of our will until we surrender ourselves to their impact.

Part One

THE
WATERSHED OF
CHANGE

2

SHIFTING
PATHS

In order to experience our watershed moments, we have to be willing to embrace change. Most of us flirt with change in a schoolgirl kind of way, running up to it and poking it, then sprinting off when it turns to look our way. I used to proudly boast, "I love change!" That was before God had me move forty-seven times in my first ten years of marriage to a professional baseball player. I sheepishly changed my proud vaunt to "Change is good only if God makes it clear he's behind it."

Change is an absolute in life, and the more we fight it or ignore it, the more it haunts us. Why do we hide from new experiences or from a truth that can set us free? Why does what we *are* look better than what we *can be*?

These are the questions I've spent the better part of thirty years poking for answers. The reason I poked them with such tenacity is that you have never seen a woman who needed to change more than I did. Insecure, lonely, destructive, people pleasing, fearful, self-loathing — and that was me on a good day. When I tearfully gave Jesus my wounded heart in college, I didn't have any lofty expectations. As a matter of fact, I didn't know much about him at all. I just knew that my life didn't work the way I was living it, and if I were to go on living, it had to change. But change never comes easy. Initially resting on God's bosom came easy, but the process of changing my messy mind has been like watching oak trees grow — you don't notice they've grown until you're sitting under their shade.

Often the watershed of change is preceded by a period of feeling stuck. Making the same bad choices over and over; struggling with a poor self-image; being trapped in a destructive relationship; feeling bored, poor, sick, bland, lonely, and unloved — these are the undertones of being stuck. And it's in these undertones that I've begged God to give me his vision.

I've always been a beach lover. I'm most content when I'm looking out over a blue-tinted ripple that dazzles as the sun kisses the foamy water playing with the shore, sand in my toes, towel in my hand. I seem to be happiest when I'm frolicking inside the tow of a frisky wave. But when I asked God to teach me about change and the process of leaving the stuck for the unstuck, he simply replied, "You need to think about the mountains."

Growing up in Colorado, I've spent most of my life in the shadow of the Rockies. My childhood was full of mountains, as my grandparents lived in a town nuzzled deep in the rhythm of the mountains' sway. But still I resisted. "I don't want to think of mountains," I chided. "I want to think of the beach. Mountains are too hard."

No matter how much I argued, the same images came forth. Our epiphany moments of watershed demand a response, and that response is like climbing a mountain. Watersheds lead us to change, and change can feel like the upward trudge of boots on rocky terrain.

Mountains *are* hard. They're steep, unpredictable, and often dangerous, but the view from the peak's summit is the view that God wants all of us to possess — the view of clarity, the view of transformation, and the view of trust. So with towel and beach chair behind me, I vowed to learn everything I could about God's beckon to climb.

This isn't a physical mountain you stand at the base of, but rather a spiritual mountain that every lover of God must acknowledge. Respectfully, God doesn't tell us to climb a mountain and then leave us to fend for ourselves. He gives us a team to travel with, capable guides to walk beside us and, if necessary, to hold us until we become strong on our feet. He introduces our guides as Faith, Hope, and Humility.

Faith stands in front of us with sure footing and a lantern. Rugged and strong, Faith is in great shape. He's trained and ready for mountain climbing, which is a relief to those of us whose muscles might need a little more time at the gym. Whenever it gets dark and we can't see, Faith is the hand we take hold of.

Behind us is *Humility*. When we're tempted to run from change — or slink away from Faith's leading — Humility holds us in place, reminding us that our strength will increase as we trust the One who has invited us to change. Humility isn't handsome, like a face you'd see on the cover of a magazine, but there's a unique attractiveness to his form. He's selfless and assured, always ready to think of us before himself, which can be quite a chore when you're dealing with novice mountain climbers.

Hope is the one we talk to. Because he is next to us, it's his arm that we often grab when the dirt under our feet begins to give way. He's good at conversation and helps keep our minds off the difficult challenges change brings.

After the insight of a watershed moment, part of my problem with instituting change is that I feel tired before I even begin. I stand at the base of the mountain and start to mumble in panic, "I can't do this. It's too hard! Change is for other people who are stronger than I am." It's here that Faith turns around and looks into my eyes, Humility puts a hand on my back, and Hope says, "You can. You will. You must."

CHANGE AND SURRENDER

Though mountain climbing may have a rugged romanticism to it, there's nothing romantic about change. Change is for grown-ups; it's for those willing to be honest with themselves and shed attitudes, behaviors, and beliefs that keep them from fresh watershed moments with God.

Children typically change because they're told to *speak politely, be tidy, be respectful, do their homework, brush their teeth, be good friends.* We dictate our measures of change to our children and then provide helpers — parents, siblings, teachers, mentors — to assist them with the changes we hope to see.

Adults, however, usually change because they need to, not because they want to. They recognize that to move forward in their lives — spiritually, physically, and emotionally — they're going to have to learn new behaviors and new ways of making sense of what they know.

According to educator Malcolm Knowles, adults have a strong readiness to learn things that help them cope with daily life effectively, but they have to know *why* they should learn something before they'll invest the time.[3] I regularly talk to men and women who repeat lines as if they've auditioned with the same monologues for the better part of their adult life:

"This is the way I've always been. It's my personality."

"I've gotten along just fine this way. I see no need to change!"

"I don't like the way they do things over there. It's not what I'm familiar with."

"I may not be perfect, but I'm better than most people I know."

These types of comments keep us stuck in cycles of monotony or despair. I know a lot about these cycles because I tossed about in them for years, like a washing machine eternally set on spin.

After a tragic car accident that left my dad paralyzed from the neck down when I was nine, my family spiraled into chaos. Alone with three small children, medical bills, and a critically impaired husband, my mom was devastated. Alcohol became her shelter until she eventually left it for the shelter of God — but for many years our family resembled a limping soldier. We tried to battle, but our injuries left us incapacitated.

When I went to college, I knew I wasn't quite right. I couldn't figure out why I didn't want anyone to really know me. I figured they'd run for the hills when they saw how insecure I was, so I hid myself from people, and I ate. I ate and I ate and I ate. I wanted to change my destructive behavior but couldn't wrap my mind around how to change. After I got sick of eating — pants not zipping, embarrassed to be seen, feeling fat and ugly — I dieted. Dieting led to starving, and I starved myself for years, loving my sense of control but recognizing that this, too, was dangerous behavior.

When faced with the cruel fact that I was slowly killing myself, I kept trying to muster the courage to change, but I would crumble into a heap of good intentions with the same predictable results. On the verge of suicide due to my cycles of despair and hopelessness, I cried out to Jesus, begging him to prove himself real to me.

"If you're really real, Jesus," I moaned, "show yourself to me. You're the last hope I have." I wasn't in a church. I'd never heard the word *salvation*. I was just a beggar at the end of my rope, surrendering myself so God could change the course of my broken life.

Surrender is the bravest thing we'll ever do. It's the finest white flag we'll ever wave. It's the catalyst that allows our watershed moments to emerge.

PATHS OF SURRENDER

Often when authors talk about moments with God, they speak as if these moments present themselves at a one-size-fits-all bargain sale — here's the rack you should look at if you need advice; here's the rack you peruse when you need healing; here's the rack you comb through to grow. With no trip to the dressing room to see if they fit, we end up with a load in our arms that may not be right for us at all!

Sadly, I've walked around for years with someone else's tailor-fit outfit clinging loosely to my spirit's shape and form. What a joy it is to shed that outfit and realize that God is much more creative in his design for us than one-size-fits-all. As we shed dogma and directives that might not be meant for us, it frees us to look at what *is* meant for us — a distinct, exclusive invitation to surrender who we are to a God who loves us.

Because God is uniquely sketching our lives, each of us will take different paths toward the watershed of change. For some the path may be rocky, for others it may be barren, and for some it may look like the dead-end wall of a canyon. These paths are meant to be walked on, traveled on, and camped on; they're not paths we visit once and never return to. Surrender is a path we'll continue to travel until we take our last breath on earth. If we're committed to growth, we'll cross these paths repeatedly on the way to our spiritual summit.

The *rocky path* of surrender is the one we hear the most about. People talk about these rocks; we rally around these rocks; we cry for people trapped by these rocks — and try as we may, it's impossible to proceed past them without help. These are the multishaped boulders that stop us in our tracks: divorce, betrayal, cancer, finances, death, infertility, accidents, loss. Rocks such as these lodge themselves on our paths, taunting us to find a way around them.

The *barren path* of surrender doesn't get as much attention as the rocky path because it's harder to see what snares us in a vast path void of clarity and insight. We seem to wander on this path with no direction, excitement, or purpose. We want to feel alive, and we wonder why other people experience an intimacy with Christ that we either pretend to have or are secretly jealous that they possess. Many who travel this path have merely followed others on it since birth, listening to *their* stories of loving God but never experiencing stories uniquely their own.

Finally we come to the *dead-end path* of surrender, a path that leads smack into the walls of a canyon. No matter which way we turn, solid rock shoots straight up. There's no way out. No escape. This is the path of addiction, rebellion, and prodigal promises that whisper life but instead bring death.

Each of these paths leads to the same outcome — to continue to change we must surrender. We can try to maneuver around the rocks, pretend we don't feel barren, or look for ways to escape the foreboding walls of a canyon — but a heartfelt cry to Jesus will lift us from these paths and set us on a new path that's clear of obstruction and vitally alive.

Sometimes I surrender with a clear mind and a strong voice, able to articulate what I need to move forward and my desire to be led to new heights with God. Other times I can't even speak. I'm too weary, confused, hurt, or deceived. I seem to crawl spiritually, inch by inch, until I sense my surrender lifting me from the ground to my feet.

Truthfully, isn't that all God asks of us? A heart surrendered to his help and glory? Isn't it time we traded our lives in the suburbs for a mountain where God's voice breathes like the song of the wildflowers? The funny thing about mountain flowers is that the higher you get, the more you realize no one will ever see these remarkable fields of jewels. It's as if they were created for God's eyes alone.

What a joy it is to realize that, like those flowers, we don't change so that we will be noticed by others. We don't change out of guilt or duty, but rather for the sheer pleasure of learning the ways of God. We know he will acknowledge our courage, even if no one else does.

3

HIDING
IN CAVES

Why do watershed moments that hold promise for change send us into hiding? What is it about hiding that seems safer than changing? Could it be that in our hope for change, sometimes we need to retreat when the moments of growth are relentless and demanding? Sometimes we need a place to catch our breath and think. What we need is a cave.

In high school, one of my friends invited a few people to go rock climbing with him. I didn't know this boy very well, but it seemed like a fabulous idea to me. Never mind the fact that we didn't have a stitch of proper equipment or that I knew nothing about climbing rocks. We piled into his car and headed for some mountains just outside of Denver. We pulled our car to the side of the road and craned our necks as we looked up at the rocks beside the highway.

"Cool …" was my response, which probably should have sounded more like, "No way …" But given my rosy reaction to most things in life, *cool* was truly how I was feeling.

My girlfriends and I had on sneakers (I'm surprised we weren't wearing flip-flops), and our rock climbing buddy had on boots. So we began our climb. No ropes, no gear, no nothing — just sneakers against the steep wall of rust-colored mountain rock and gravel. After an hour, I looked below and was startled by the cars speeding by on the highway beneath us. One small slip or jolt would send us tumbling down into the mix of traffic. I finally felt scared.

I knew we couldn't go any higher, but I didn't want to seem like a chicken, and it was at that precise moment that we saw a cave. Close enough for us to settle into, the walls of the mountain met, forming a protective pocket in the rocks. As I collapsed onto the floor of the cave, I wasn't chanting "cool" but rather "thank you" as I prayed a silent prayer of relief. We sat in that cave until the traffic died down, stirring up the nerve to descend the rocks with what little strength we had left.

Ever since that day, I've been a lover of caves. Caves can provide shelter, relief, or a place to hide when we're not yet ready to live outside of them. I'm reminded of the emotional caves I've crawled into when I wasn't sure how to proceed or was too tired to move forward.

In the process of change, sometimes it's tempting to sprint toward the highest peaks, to run toward a complete overhaul of ourselves with a zeal that ends in burnout. But God often leads us to a cave to teach us some skills before we ascend, skills to enhance our efforts and protect us from the frustration of wanting to change but feeling as though the results don't come fast enough.

One of the most profound watershed moments in the Bible takes place in a cave. It's a moment in which David is stunned by the weight of humility, a prerequisite to any change that makes a difference in our lives. In order to change, we must humbly admit we need to. For any perfect people, any perfect lovers of humanity and God, your work is done. But for the rest of us who flounder between good intent and reality, a cave is a welcome place where we can learn.

Formerly a shepherd, David was used to spacious night skies and forest-lined hills, but he found himself hiding deep within a cave — fearful, confused, and disappointed in a king he had revered and trusted.

Most people think this is a story about jealousy — King Saul jealous of the up-and-coming hype of Israel, David. But it's about something much more than jealousy; it's about the redemptive gift of humility that ushers in change.

I'm ashamed to admit I've often left this gift unwrapped, sitting on a table decorated with lush greenery, flowers, and fragrant candles. Give me the beauty of the decorated table, but not the gift that sits on it. For David, humility would be the box he'd continue to unwrap, the gift he'd continue to prize — the watershed that enhanced his wisdom and his desperate need for God.

From sheepherder to anointed hero, David's life turned upside down when he killed the Philistine giant Goliath. In the same moment, Israel's King Saul felt a gut punch because of the attention this young hero received.

> When the men were returning home after David had killed the Philistine, the women came out from all the towns of Israel to meet King Saul with singing and dancing, with joyful songs and with timbrels and lyres. As they danced, they sang:
>
> "Saul has killed his thousands,
>   and David his tens of thousands."
>
> Saul was very angry; this refrain displeased him greatly. "They have credited David with tens of thousands," he thought, "but me with only thousands. What more can he get but the kingdom?" And from that time on Saul kept a close eye on David.
>
> 1 SAMUEL 18:6 – 9

All it took was a chant from women on the side of the road to cause Saul to lose all sense of dignity. It wasn't reports from the military or meetings with his advisers that brought on this insecurity; it was simply women admiring someone other than himself. If you've ever been a victim of jealousy's blows, you know it's fueled by irrational thinking — which is something like trying to talk sense to an unruly toddler.

What's interesting about Saul's jealousy toward David is that it's unwarranted. It's not like Saul wasn't gifted and blessed. To start with, he was gorgeous: "a choice and handsome man, and there was not a more handsome person than he among the sons of Israel; from his shoulders and up he was taller than any of the people" (1 Samuel 9:2 NASB).

I can't imagine a more flattering description. He's choice; he's tall; he's handsome — more handsome than anyone else. Seriously, ladies, does it get any better than that? And if that wasn't enough to fuel an ego for a lifetime, he was blessed by God.

For those tempted to lump Saul into an "unchurched loser" category, it's surprising to study the intense moments with God he'd had earlier in his life. Saul was chosen and anointed by the prophet Samuel; the Spirit of the Lord came upon him powerfully; God changed him into a new man; and he spoke words of prophecy along with the prophets of his youth (1 Samuel 10). He sounds more like a charming prince than a jealous king. He had everything, but he became obsessed with something he couldn't possibly have — the admiration and adoration of everyone he encountered. That's the tricky thing about jealousy — it doesn't operate with a fair set of rules. Jealousy wants to win, and it doesn't care who it hurts to end up on top.

The spring before my senior year, it was time for the annual ritual of varsity cheerleading tryouts. Always a painful endeavor, the tryouts at our school were especially tough because the coaches packed the entire student body into a huge gymnasium to watch us move, one by one, to the center of the gym, like sheep ready for slaughter. First, we had to do a gymnastic run consisting of a front handspring, round-off, cartwheel, and the splits. For those of us who aren't inclined to flip ourselves upside down from a running sprint on a hard gym floor with no mats, the idea of a front handspring is as crazy as eating fire. Not once in all the months I practiced for this fateful day did I nail the front handspring. Not once.

Shortly before it was my turn, I found myself kneeling under the bleachers where the student body had gathered. I wasn't a prayerful person at the time, but I prayed the most heartfelt prayer you can imagine.

"Dear God, you know my family has struggled greatly, and I'm really insecure. I realize I haven't come to you much, but if you could help me do my best and be satisfied whether I make this team or not, I would be so grateful. Actually, could you please just help me make it? Amen!"

Blazing across the floor I entered into my front handspring. Boom! I landed flat on my bottom as the student body gasped a sigh of embarrassment. Resolutely, I finished the rest of the stunts and stood in the middle of the gym to do my cheers. After the audition, the student body went into private booths to vote for their six varsity cheerleaders for the next year.

We didn't find out the results for two days, but when I saw my name on the list of cheerleaders, I almost fell over in excitement. That excitement soon turned to pain, however, as my closest friends who had endured the same grueling tryout on a quest to make the squad chose to ignore me when they didn't see their names on the list. When I called them on the phone, I got no answer. When I joined them at sporting events, they didn't speak to me. I was dumbfounded. I sensed that jealousy was putting a wedge between us, but I knew we loved each other too much to let it have its way.

So one day I gathered all the strength I could and told my best friend, "I hoped we could make this team together, but I want you to know there are many things I wish I had from *your* life. Two parents who are healthy and take good care of you. A safe place to come home to and invite your friends to visit. No one ever really has it all." That did it. We were instantly whole again, and the irrational pangs of jealousy were stopped in their tracks.

But for David, it would take much more than a good conversation with Saul to thwart the onslaught of jealousy. David tried to communicate with Saul, but Saul's anger spiraled from irrational to dangerous. Saul threw a spear at David, sent him to battle their archrivals the Philistines, gave David his daughter Michal as a wife to cause a snare for him politically, and eventually hunted and tracked him in the wilderness like a wild animal. David was left with no choice other than to hide.

Hiding has a bad ring to it. It reminds us of the darling ostrich who buries its head in the sand and thinks nothing bad is happening around it because it can't see it. But in David's case, hiding was productive. God led David to several caves that provided more than shelter; they provided the gift of time. Caves served as a refuge for him as he learned valuable lessons about himself, his foe, and his role as a leader.

LESSONS LEARNED IN A CAVE

When David hid himself in the cave of Adullam, a curious thing began to occur. People began to flock to him like birds trying to rebuild a nest. It seems David wasn't the only one who needed to run away: "All those who were in distress or in debt or discontented gathered around him, and he became their commander. About four hundred men were with him" (1 Samuel 22:2).

How many of us haven't at one time or another been in distress, in debt, or discontented? Distress signals being in need, in trauma, or controlled by fear. It can express itself as a turn in your health, an accident, a loss of a person or a dream. Distress makes it hard to function. No wonder these men hightailed it over to hide with David in the caves.

Some came to David drowning in debt, a type of bondage that doesn't only rear its head financially — although credit card bills are enough to make us want to hide. Debt can also take the form of habits we can't lick or addictions we're enslaved to — food, alcohol, drugs, approval. These all stink with the stench of a balance to be paid later, and that balance is usually paid in full by the loss of our peace and sanity. Debt can also be incurred when someone holds something over our heads — a guilt ransom over something we've done in the past, a threat to expose what we're afraid for people to see, or a manipulative hand of control in a relationship that's crushed by disrespect.

Then comes the quiet whimper of discontent. Sometimes it's barely audible, but you know it's there when you sense a stirring inside that life must be more than the routine grind you're attached to. You know you want to get somewhere, but you just aren't sure where or how.

It may sound like a band of misfits joined David at the cave, but truthfully I would have been at his feet in the cave too. Misery loves company, and when word got out that a man named David was camping at the stronghold near Adullam, hundreds went to join him. David was hunkered down in his cave, seeking answers and praying to God for change — change of circumstances, change of heart, change in life's annoying unfairness.

This makes me wonder about the caves *we* camp in. They may not be made of rock walls; instead they may be the walls of a bland cubicle or an inadequate paycheck. They may look like a detour from a plan we feverishly tried to carry out or like a holding pattern that seems long overdue for change. Often we think of time spent in a cave as an escape, and although we don't want to live our entire life in a cave, there are times when a cave is a place of nurturing by God. It's his hiding place — a place where he calms us, assures us, and trains us for new things. Rather than be ashamed of our caves or in a hurry to climb out of them, what if we thanked God for them?

These disheveled men's initial time in the cave must have had a profound effect on them because they soon followed David to a different cave — one located in the Desert of En Gedi and affectionately called Crags of the Wild Goats.

Cave-Dwelling Humility

If you've ever been chased by a goat, you know they can be nasty nibblers. I'll never forget seeing a goat chew the shoelaces of an unsuspecting student one day at a petting zoo. Once the goat got tired of the laces, it started to nip at the student's legs. This poor kid went screaming and crying in every direction until the zookeeper tackled the goat from behind and tied it to a post. I wonder if the name of David's new cave was somewhat prophetic. Wild goats nipping and biting can be unnerving, and what was about to happen in that cave would test every man's nerve and leave them begging to understand their situation.

We don't know much about the spiritual beliefs of the men follow-

ing David, but we do know they were watching him. They were listening to his prayers and his songs. They were studying his reactions and
his daily routines, riveted to his stories about Israel and the great King
Saul, and puzzled by the fact that he was being hunted by this same
great king. They were attracted to something inside David. His faith
teased them like candy you want to unwrap but aren't sure you'll enjoy.

One day proved to be a watershed for this formidable crew — a day
in a cave that no man was prepared for, as the king who sought to slay
David ended up in his very grasp: "So Saul took three thousand able
young men from all Israel and set out to look for David and his men
near the Crags of the Wild Goats. He came to the sheep pens along the
way; a cave was there and Saul went in to relieve himself. David and
his men were far back in the cave" (1 Samuel 24:2 – 3).

I can just picture three thousand strong men waiting outside a
cave for their leader to use the bathroom. It reminds me a bit of our
cross-country road trips. You never know when you'll end up needing
to pull over! Ironically, Saul pulled into a cave in which David and his
men were already hiding. Accidental? No way. This was God's comical
way of tying Saul's physical dung to his need for spiritual excrement.
He truly needed to relieve himself in more ways than one. David and
his men must have been biting their tongues as they watched the king
of Israel squat before them.

Now we see the personalities of the men who have spent time with
David starting to take shape. They whisper a prophecy they're sure the
Lord has crafted specifically for David:

> The men said, "This is the day the LORD spoke of when he said
> to you, 'I will give your enemy into your hands for you to deal
> with as you wish.'" Then David crept up unnoticed and cut off a
> corner of Saul's robe.
>
> 1 SAMUEL 24:4

It's easy to get caught up in personal agendas, and in this moment
David got tangled in the agenda of his men. It's true that the Lord

promised victory to David, but what if God was referring to a different type of enemy than Saul? What if he was referring to internal enemies with the names Pride and Entitlement? Bold and cocky, these enemies blow on humility with the stink of bad breath.

Truthfully, David could have been thinking, *What's Saul's problem? I can't help it if I'm popular among the people. I've earned their admiration! I'm anointed and blessed, so he needs to back off!* Pride always pushes the attention on itself, while Entitlement assures Pride it has the right to do so.

As David crawled across the cave floor to the spot where Saul's robe was laid, I wonder if it wasn't Pride and Entitlement that crept beside him. But David recognized these intruders the minute he felt the cloth of Saul's robe between his fingers. His conscience quickly broke down, and he rebuked his men, forbidding them from attacking Saul. My prideful, entitled mind would have wanted to shout out, "Are you nuts? You have every right to crush Saul!" But David was listening to a different voice, the voice of God's grace, not man's revenge. In the midst of a watershed moment, David defeated Pride and Entitlement in a victory that would define his personality for decades to come.

I'm reminded of a time when Pride and Entitlement tried to creep in beside me. Like annoying houseguests, they perched on my front porch, and then boldly forced their way into my living room. Looking back, I think they received their invitation from a messenger called Disappointment.

Bobby had been traded from the New York Yankees to the Texas Rangers during the off-season. We were thrilled because our agent had somehow negotiated the best contract we had ever signed. Coming off a few lackluster seasons with the Yankees, we happily nicknamed our agent "Houdini."

But during the last week of spring training with our new team, we were shocked to find out we had been released from the Rangers without even a ticket to the minor leagues. We were released. Banished. Sent away with no other job prospect in sight. Our agent, Houdini, now had his work cut out for him as he told us to get to Los Angeles as quickly as we could. This was no small task, considering we were living in the southern tip of Florida, but off we went with our van packed to the ceiling around our two daughters, two and three years of age. To make matters worse, I was newly pregnant and sick around the clock. We drove fourteen hours a day on our quest to reach Los Angeles, and the moment we crossed the California state line our agent called to let us know we had a new contract ready to be signed — shortstop for the Pittsburgh Pirates' top minor league team in Buffalo, New York! I moaned when I thought about joining Bobby in yet another corner of the country, but several days after he flew out to join the team, I left California to reunite with him, morning sickness crackers in hand.

He rented a place for us before I arrived, and as I entered the apartment, the first thing I noticed were the bugs. They seemed to be crawling all over the kitchen counters, family room walls, even on the beds. "*Lovely,*" I thought. "*We're sharing this space with so many of God's creatures.*" One day I went to load the dishwasher, and as I opened the door, it fell off its hinges and smashed my toes! It seemed that every day something was going wrong in that place. I've never gotten so close to an apartment manager in all my life.

The ballpark was no better. It had been a while since we had played in the minor leagues, and the first thing I noticed was the silly activities throughout the games — a far cry from games in Yankee Stadium. One night they froze the tops of the dugouts with sheets of ice. There were literally ice skaters twirling on top of the dugouts.

I sat in an exhausted tangle as I reviewed the events of the last few months. We had fallen from shortstop on the most elite team in the world to shortstop for a team with frozen dugout roofs. Pride and Entitlement were screaming in my ears with gale force: *This is ridiculous. You are so much better than this! You don't belong here; this is way beneath you.* I wish I could say I pushed these two intruders immediately off my mental playground, but I insisted on playing with them for a while before they began to offend me.

I began to sense the Lord trying to speak to me, but Pride and Entitlement made it hard to listen — until one day God possessively grabbed me and spoke in my wax-filled ears.

"I want you to start a Bible study."

I shot back a response. "You can't mean me. I have the worst attitude, I have nothing positive to say, and I might embarrass you, Lord!"

God seemed to laugh at my retort and simply said, "I *do* mean you. Let's get moving." I reluctantly agreed out of sheer obedience.

The thing about playing ball in the top minor league affiliate for a major league team was that it was filled with players and wives who felt just like I did. Many had tasted the sweet life of the major leagues and were frantically trying to claw their way back. One wife on our team was particularly outspoken. She was nicknamed "Dragon Woman" because she was so quick to snarl at anyone who tried to reach out to her. Her husband had a few weeks under his belt in the major leagues, which we referred to as "having a cup of coffee." A taste like that is more of a tease than anything else. Like drinking a full-roast blend and then being forced to drink instant coffee when you're sent back down to the minors, one good cup always leaves you wanting more. Because of his lukewarm big league appearance, he was shuffled back to the minors, and she made sure everyone knew how unhappy they were about it! Every wife on our team was afraid of her, including me, so when I ended up in the back of a van she was driving as she transported all the wives to the ballpark one day, I painfully knew this was my chance to invite Dragon Woman and the other wives to a Bible study. When I mentioned I would be hosting a Bible study in my apartment over the weekend, an awkward silence fell over the van. I was ready to open the door of our overstuffed vehicle and limp alongside the highway when suddenly Dragon Woman responded.

"What's the study about?" she asked.

"It's about disappointments and bad attitudes, and how God can turn them into something good," I said.

"I'll be there!" she barked out, and I promise that every woman in that van had to pull her jaw off the floor.

Our Bible study that summer proved to be one of the most powerful I've ever experienced. Every wife on the team came — even the Spanish-speaking wives who didn't understand a word I was saying. One wife called me in a panic after her husband got called to join the major league team in Pittsburgh. She planned a quick trip back to Buffalo just to pray with me to receive Jesus as her Savior, then rejoined the team in Pittsburgh! She could have prayed that prayer anywhere — she didn't need me to pray it — but she just wanted to be in my arms when she prayed, and that was more meaningful to me than ten years in the big leagues.

It was breathtaking to note that God took my pride and entitlement and replaced them with the strength of humility. This was my watershed moment, a rush of humble surrender that led to a watershed of change. Although we never made it back to the major leagues after that season, my attitude from that day forward was never the same.

Bent by Humility

Humility typically isn't described as "strong"; it tends to be viewed as "mild" and "mousy." But the truth is, nothing rivals the strength of humility, because those who are trained by it have worked out their faith with vigor and tenacity. Humility is power dressed in grace.

Sometimes humility hits like a cyclone. Before you know it, you're flailing and thrashing in circumstances beyond your control. You're being twisted. You're being broken. You're being bent.

In 1904, a young man named Ethan Roberts prayed the type of prayer that brings forth change. As a teenager living in Wales, Ethan began to pray that his country would seek God. After praying for a decade, he recognized hardness in his own heart, yearning for change but languishing in the monotony of routine belief. One day he heard someone pray three words that distinctly inspired him: "Lord, bend us." The next night in a prayer meeting he knelt and begged the Lord, "Bend me! Bend me!" — and God did. From that day forward, everything changed. Ethan had come to his watershed.

Ethan and his friends began to ask for one hundred thousand souls to come to salvation. On Monday night, October 31, 1904, Ethan brought this four-point message to his home church at Loughor, Wales:

1. Is there any sin in your past that you have not confessed to God? On your knees at once. Your past must be put away, and your self cleansed.
2. Is there anything in your life that is doubtful — anything you cannot decide whether it is good or evil? Away with it. There must not be a cloud between you and God.
3. Do what the Holy Spirit prompts you to do. Obey promptly, implicitly, and with unquestioning submission to God's Spirit.
4. Publicly profess Christ as your Savior.

Ethan's cry became "bend the church and save the world" — and once again, God answered his prayer. As a matter of public record in 1904, sinful habits began to wane in Wales. Taverns closed, gambling businesses lost their trade, and brothels locked their doors. Families were reunited and broken friendships were reconciled; old debts were paid and forgiveness for past offenses flowed; stolen goods were returned and profanity ceased. Divisions in churches were healed; denominational and class barriers were broken down; feuds were forgotten; discord and enmity were replaced by peace and harmony and unity.

Attendance at meetings began to grow, and the movement spread to other towns and villages. Names of converts were sent to the newspapers. After two months, seventy thousand people had come to Christ, and ultimately one hundred thousand confessed faith in Jesus Christ.[4] All this transpired from three words prayed from a humble bow: "Lord, bend us."

I've made this my personal creed. "Bend me" is how I begin my day. It's how I enter meetings and conversations that make me nervous. It's how I interact with friends and how I love my husband and kids. If we are bent, we are pliable. And pliable believers are treasured in God's classroom.

One night, I was driving my friend Courtney home from a meeting when she suddenly grew quiet. "I've got something to tell you," she whispered, as if she didn't know where to start. "Just start from the beginning," I offered as I pulled to the side of the curb to listen. She began to tell her story as little streams fell from her moist eyes.

"I think back to a day in the late 1980s when I was still a teenager. Standing alone in the front yard of our home, I was watching as a team of men dug up our azalea bushes. We had about twenty bushes that bloomed in our yard, and in the stifling heat I remember being sad, distraught, and heartbroken. These men were digging up our bushes because as a last resort my mother had sold them. Our house was emptied of almost everything, and now our front yard was empty too.

"I remember having a lot of stress and worry — heavy loads for a young person. But I had been an adult for a long time. My mother was a single parent, and I was her only child. I carried life's burdens alongside her. I had done so for years, and it was me she confided in. I had full visibility to life's storms before I was experienced enough to carry an umbrella.

"I remember thinking about my mom sitting inside the house while I was standing in the yard watching our bushes being stripped away. She was hiding in humiliation, insecurity, and failure. My mother's value was tied up in that house, that yard, which private school she could send me to, which exclusive camp I could attend in the summer. As our life crumbled around us, she felt worthless, drowning in a river of despair that she couldn't climb out of. As the child, I looked to her for courage, strength, and security, but she had none. She had none because she didn't have *him* — she didn't have Jesus.

"On Valentine's Day, twenty-two years later, I was on the phone with a friend when the doorbell rang. A FedEx guy handed me a package from an attorney. I assured myself it was just another notice from a creditor. My husband lost his job in 2009 and was out of work for fourteen months. During that time we exhausted all our savings, retirement, and credit just trying to survive our lifestyle — *our value.*

"As I read the letter, I felt my chest getting tight. I was standing there just as I was twenty-two years earlier in the yard. Time stopped. 'It looks like we're being foreclosed on,' I calmly said to my friend, and then I hung up the phone.

"I was back in that front yard, only this time I was my mother — humiliated, exposed, worthless. I was terrified for our children, our future, and our marriage. What would everyone think? How would I explain? How could I forgive my husband for the financial secrets he'd been keeping from me?

"I remembered my mother as I felt stupid, out of control, and reckless in the way I had trusted my husband. I thought about all the times she warned me that I would be heartbroken and betrayed by a man, just like she was. I felt like screaming, 'I don't want this! This isn't supposed to happen to me again. I should have never quit working. I should have never trusted a man to take care of me and our children!'

"And then I felt it. His peace. His love. His assurance. Jesus reminded me that I am a child of God — I have him — and that's enough. I will not follow my mother's footsteps into bitterness, misery, and struggle. I will not let my children down. I will trust him, and I will forgive as I have been forgiven, resting on the courage and hope of my Savior."

At forty-one years of age, Courtney experienced a watershed moment in which humility tutored her in the grace of forgiveness, trust, and love. She is wildly free. She has hope for her future and her marriage, and a true understanding of her worth.

The other day, Courtney and I had a sweet conversation in which she shared, "It's been four months since we moved into our

1,400-square-foot apartment with our dog, two children, and remnants of the life we had before. We affectionately nicknamed our apartment 'The Bend,' because it's been in these circumstances that God has bent us, and that's a bending I willingly submit to. When he bends me, that's when I'm made straight."

Humility's Squeeze

What I love most about David's life is that he never stopped asking the Lord to bend him. Never are we more bent than when we sit within humility's grasp and tell it to squeeze. It was in this squeezing that David, still crouched in the cave, whispered these words to his men about the king who was hunting him: "The Lord forbid that I should do such a thing to my master, the Lord's anointed, or lay my hand on him; for he is anointed of the Lord" (1 Samuel 24:6).

David recognized a plan and authority at work that was greater than him. The same prophet Samuel who had anointed and commissioned Saul had also anointed and commissioned David. But David didn't cling to accolades or spiritual résumés; he clung to the hope of God. And it was in this hope that he stood outside the cave and called out to Saul after the king had exited the cave unharmed:

> Then David went out of the cave and called out to Saul, "My lord the king!" When Saul looked behind him, David bowed down and prostrated himself with his face to the ground. He said to Saul, "Why do you listen when men say, 'David is bent on harming you?' This day you have seen with your own eyes how the Lord delivered you into my hands in the cave. Some urged me to kill you, and I spared you; I said, 'I will not lay my hand on my lord, because he is the Lord's anointed.'"
>
> 1 Samuel 24:8–10

I can picture David looking up at Saul, his face stained by dirt from prostrating himself, humbly expressing the truth that had welled inside him for months. But humility isn't weak; it doesn't stutter — and David faced his adversary with commanding eloquence.

His men were huddled behind him as he spoke, ready to spring into action should Saul make a wrong move. They watched their leader waive his right to retaliation. They watched him crawl and prostrate himself like an unworthy servant. I believe that in this moment *they* experienced a watershed moment that would leave them profoundly changed too.

The caves they lived in provided more than a hiding place; they were the womb that birthed a newly born outlook diapered in humble submission. This watershed of change can only be experienced when a few essentials are in place: belief, trust, and obedience. Each of these must be present for change to take place.

Belief: Belief is the substance of growth, and growth can't flourish if we don't believe the God who grows it. God revealed his character to David and his men by nudging David to crawl, not strut. Every man watching this encounter was changed, including David himself. It's here that belief matures. When we're tempted to push out, stand out, or shout out, the wisest response may be to revert to crawling, a humble crawling that leads us to the lap of God.

Trust: This desert group of distressed, discontented debtors had been learning to trust a God who seemed invisible. They had listened to David pray. They had followed him into battle, and in the cave with Saul they watched him trust God rather than brandish his sword in revenge. These men came to the caves fearful, wild, and scared of their future.

But trust crushes fear when we let it, for we learn to trust through what we fear. Ponder this: What scares you more than anything? What fear holds your heart in a paralyzed grip, causing it to go limp — losing your kids, the death of a spouse, cancer, being unable to pay your bills?

I used to line up my fears and label them from worse to absolutely intolerable. The worst were fears that had to do with being married to a ballplayer, and the intolerable focused on pain that could ensue in my children's lives. I can confidently say I have lived through every one of the fears I imagined in my youth, and you know what? I'm still standing, still believing, and still loving my God. Trust kills fear, freeing us from cowering in fear's bullying shadow.

Obedience: Belief and trust have no power or relevance if we don't obey what they teach us. What God shows us in the caves, we need to live out in the meadows. Our obedience will have a far-reaching influence over other cave dwellers and those who watch our lives with hopeful expectation.

David's humility not only changed his men, but the man who sought to destroy him. When David finished speaking to Saul outside the cave, Saul responded with words that echoed the raw wounds of his insecure heart: "'Is that your voice, David my son?' And he wept aloud. 'You are more righteous than I,' he said. 'You have treated me well, but I have treated you badly'" (1 Samuel 24:16–17).

This stately king weeps as he speaks to the man he's trying to kill. And it's not any man; it's a man he calls "son." Humility has left its imprint as we hear Saul express his pain: "You are a better man than I." When you've smelled someone's humility, you're left with a reflective question with a scent of its own. "How am *I* doing? Am I capable of pushing myself to the background to let God fulfill a greater purpose?"

Sadly, Saul would continue to hunt David, but that day he experienced the weight of humility, and its brawn didn't stop there. David's men changed too. As a matter of fact, it was through their humiliating time in caves that they learned to be mighty. This same group of cave-dwelling losers soon became the army of King David, which would later be referred to as "the mighty men" (2 Samuel 10:7 NASB).

The caves they spent time in proved to be more than places to hide; they proved to be the training ground for humble might. We don't need to run from our caves; we need to be trained by them.

Part Two

THE
WATERSHED OF
AWARENESS

4

UNRAVELING KNOTS
OF DYSFUNCTION

When I was a teen, one summer day, out of sheer boredom a few of my neighbors gathered on the concrete floor of my garage to cut into the middle of a baseball to see what was inside. Using the sharp end of a pocketknife we sliced through the smooth cowhide exterior and unraveled yards upon yards of tightly wound string. It wasn't until the floor of the garage was covered in a small hill of twine that we got to the center of the ball. Like the cream filling on the inside of a Twinkie, we found a tiny rubber sphere — the essential ingredient to making a baseball fly. Without the string tightly encasing that sphere, a baseball will never soar.

We spend countless amounts of money, time, and energy keeping our lives tightly wound in a neat display of sufficiency, but what happens when they start to unravel? What's at the center of our ball? It's when we cut through the smooth exterior of our lives that we can experience a watershed of awareness and reveal what has us wound so tight. Ironically, unraveling the layers of our lives — the way we've processed the experiences of our youth and the strategies we've employed to help make sense of things — can help our lives soar.

When I was growing up, Friday night was by far the best night of the week. This was the night that boasted back-to-back TV sitcoms,

The Brady Bunch and *The Partridge Family*. I was so in love with these shows that it hurt. At one point, I actually wanted to be both Marsha Brady and Laurie Partridge. I wore my hair stick straight and parted in the middle (no small job for a girl with naturally curly hair!). But what struck me most about these families is that they never seemed to unravel. They handled every situation with humor and a plan that took exactly thirty minutes to resolve. By the time the end credits were rolling, everyone was once again happy, healthy, and loving each other well.

Before *The Brady Bunch* and *The Partridge Family* there was a show so popular it's still quoted from today — *Leave It to Beaver*. Beaver was always getting into mischief, and his older brother, Wally, would roll his eyes in amazement at his brother's mishaps.

I recently saw a rerun of an episode of this black-and-white classic and was stunned by its innocence and family portrayal. Beaver had disobeyed his parents and went to the movies when they said not to. While at the movies he won a prize — a new bike! The episode ended with him confessing this indiscretion to his father and mother, who both sat attentively as they listened to their son tearfully explain his misbehavior. He told them the truth and then shared how he already took the bike and donated it to the church down the street because he knew he wasn't worthy of it. His parents agreed he had done the right thing, and then laid out a punishment for him (no more movies for the next few weeks) so he would learn his lesson.

My eyes opened wide as I thought about how different my experience was as I grew up. I don't remember sitting together as a family for many endearing conversations, and I would have lied about where I got the new bike and would have hoped to cover it up so I could keep it. So much for innocent family drama in our home growing up!

After watching this show, I was tempted to think that families long ago really got it right. But God reminded me that even the first family recorded in history, Adam and Eve's, had problems with family drama. Their "pristine" family's two sons, Cain and Abel, fought like crazy, and their interactions ended in crime and heartbreak. Even after Cain killed his brother, he smugly shouted to God, "Am I my brother's keeper?" when God tried to help him. Maybe we're not so messed up after all.

I believe most young parents start a family intending to provide a good life for them. If you've come from a loving home, you try to emulate the love and values you grew up with. If you've come from a hurting home, you've probably prayed to do better. God places us in families so we can be nurtured and encouraged until we're ready to thrive on our own. We are neither bound by our family's imperfections nor necessarily coddled by their enduring love. Families are God's nests in which we *grow in* and then *fly from*. We were never meant to live our entire lives in a nest; we were created to fly. But for some, the nests we were raised in have somehow clipped our wings, keeping us "nestbound" instead of heading skyward.

KNOTS OF DYSFUNCTION

The watershed of awareness can be described as the gifted moments in which you understand why you act or react the way you do. Sometimes these moments come in an instant, like the flood of a memory that unlocks a door. Other times they unfold like the slow pulse of the seasons — at first dark, cold, and misty, until sunshine clears the sky and warms the air. Once we receive these moments, we are better equipped to explore the mysteries of our behavior, attitudes, and outlook.

If watershed moments leave us changed, there's a good chance we'll need some tools to help us unravel the awareness this change brings. Earlier I likened change to a steep climb up a mountain. And for anyone courageous enough to climb, anything that helps is a gift.

I've been told that ropes are the most useful tool for those who climb. A rope is the one essential that has no replacement, but a rope has no purpose if we don't learn to fasten and unfasten knots. Some knots hold our rope in place while we move past difficult stretches of terrain, while other knots tied in the wrong places get tighter the more we pull on them, rendering our ropes useless. These last knots are the ones that need to be unraveled so our rope can be stretched and fulfill its purpose.

Sometimes life inside a family is like living with knots. The more we try to untie them, the more we make the knots worse. These are the knots of dysfunction, favoritism, ignorance, and generational poor choices. Most rope lovers will tell you that to get rid of unwanted kinks, you have to diligently go to the center of the knot and work from there to set in motion the process of unraveling. One construction worker offered this advice to someone who couldn't free their rope of unwanted knots: "Move the ends of the rope near the knot back and forth, side to side, until you see the knot loosening a little. Try working the knot in the reverse direction of the rope. Separate fibers without cutting anything. Stick something smack in the middle of the knot and loosen it up."

Sometimes I think the thing I stuck smack in the middle of my knots was my sanity. But it's been worth the loosening when I've stood back to observe the capable hand of peace moving back and forth to unravel me. Thankfully I come from a line of sturdy knot unravelers. It's not easy to untangle knots, but as I've watched my mom's commitment to unfastening her own knots, I've begun to understand some of my own kinks and the need for unfettered rope as I learn to overcome dysfunction.

For years I was consumed with untying the knots of my life — angry that my rope had gotten snarled by others in ways I had no control over, and upset that I had tied some nasty knots of my own on the rope I so desperately needed to climb. It's easy to see our ropes get tangled among the ropes of our parents, spouse, children, and siblings; and before we know it, we're snarled in a heap. It's the healthy climber who learns to respect the ropes around them without getting twisted by other people's knots.

I once heard a wise woman say, "If you want to understand who you are, you need to explore who you've come from." It took me years to finally begin to apply this wisdom. I had wandered around trying to figure out what was wrong with me. Why did I react to things the way I did? Why did I feel so distant from those I longed to love? My mom and I have gracefully settled into a place of love and respect, but it wasn't until I understood *her* stories and the knots she had to untie that I began to understand my own quest for clarity.

My mom's father (my grandfather) was the sixth child of an Irish immigrant who had bravely left her home in Ireland to start a life in America. I remember rubbing my hands over a weathered trunk that held her belongings. I've always wondered how you pack for a journey like that — a journey with no return ticket stub.

When she arrived in the United States, she married a Scottish stonemason who battled alcoholism. They were poor and had struggled so much that although my grandfather had an IQ bordering on genius, he failed second grade because he didn't have shoes to wear to school. Because of the pain of poverty and alcohol in his childhood, my grandfather tried to shelter his own family from any mistakes or harm. He didn't want his children to do anything that might hinder their progress in life, but this overprotective cloak prohibited my mom from standing on her own two feet or developing any of the coping skills she would need later as her life began to unfold.

Mom's mother was the eighth child born into a farming family that lived in a wooden cabin in the quiet hills of Virginia. She and her twin sister left the cabin at the age of seventeen to explore the big city of Washington, DC. There she met my grandfather, and they married. At age eighteen, she gave birth to my mom, and two years later a son was born. I'll let my mom tell the rest in her own words:

"It wasn't long before my mom began to suffer from what she called nervous breakdowns. She had about seven or eight of these, and it took years to recover from them. The remedy was shock therapy, and my dad had to stop everything when the breakdowns occurred.

His mother had died in a mental hospital, and he wasn't going to let that happen to his wife.

"My mother loved a home and clothes. She didn't get involved with things that made her nervous. She never drove. She didn't pay bills. She rarely went to the store. It was terrifying to watch these breakdowns, and my way of coping was to be perfect for my father and take care of everything that might upset my mother. My mother was a simple woman, but a woman of great faith. Eventually she found the right treatment for her mental illness and had good years with my dad before facing the challenges of widowhood with remarkable courage. It was after my husband's car accident — that fateful night his car rolled off a stretch of highway leaving him paralyzed from the neck down — that I realized she was the only person I wanted around me in the aftermath of my own family's heartache. She was a simple woman, but she understood pain. She deeply loved me, and I think that's why I felt safe with her and no one else.

"My drinking began after the accident. I had no concept of growth or faith, no tools for coping. I thought that women went crazy, had breakdowns — so I numbed myself with alcohol to prevent that from happening. But alcohol wasn't the real issue; not believing I could stand on my own two feet was. It took me years to realize I could make it, and this was the fear and anger I wrestled with. For a time I disliked my parents, blaming them for my inadequacies, but through the lessons I learned in Alcoholics Anonymous after I decided to fully surrender my life to God, I realized they truly loved me and had bestowed on me a legacy of survival. I learned to survive from watching their lives — their inner strength. I learned to surrender by embracing their imperfections and grace."

Watching my mom bravely unravel her knots helped me untie my own. Often we get stuck blaming our parents for the mistakes they've made rather than respecting the work they've done to scale their own mountains. Sadly, I've witnessed more women than I can count snarled in a bitter heap, repeating the same old "blame chants" toward their parents, refusing to move beyond the injustices of their childhood. I've spent time in that bitter heap myself, and I'm certain it never helps us change. Bitterness is like ticks in the forest that burrow under our flesh and cause disease, often going unnoticed if we fail to search for the places they like to hide.

When I went away to college, more than my address changed, and I returned to Colorado from my first year at San Diego State University in love with Jesus in ways I couldn't explain. I know I scared more than a few people with my hurricane-like fervor for a Savior who saved my life — literally. When I read that "if anyone is in Christ, the new creation has come: The old has gone, the new is here!" (2 Corinthians 5:17), I ran away and eloped with this Scripture. I thought I could escape from who I was and from a past I couldn't make sense of. Although I'm grateful for the new life this Scripture promises, years later my childhood snuck up on me and forced me to face it. More important, it forced me to feel it, because I had run from it long enough.

One Sunday, Bobby and I were asked to be guest speakers at a worship service in our large home church while he was playing for the New York Yankees. We prayerfully prepared our message and went on stage to speak. The audience was engaged and hanging on every word when suddenly I was compelled to share a story that had flashed into my mind.

We had been sharing about moments in our lives — watersheds, if you will — that had left a stark impression on our faith when we were young. When Bobby was done speaking, it was my turn, and being a natural talker, I grabbed the microphone like someone grabbing a trophy. I began to share a memory of Christmas Day a few years after my dad's car accident. I was eleven years old at the time, and my eight-year-old sister and five-year-old brother and I were excited about this day of presents and joy.

Early that Christmas Day, the physical therapist who lived with my dad dropped him off at our home to spend Christmas with us.

Mom began drinking early, and in her sad frustration, she started to hit my dad. Eventually he fell out of his wheelchair into a helpless heap on the floor. My sister, brother, and I tried to lift him back into his chair, but he was deadweight in our small arms, so for the remainder of Christmas Day he sprawled in the hallway leading to our kitchen. We showed him our toys and walked around him until the therapist came to get him around eight o'clock that evening. Late that night, I realized we hadn't eaten dinner, and after a peek in the oven revealed a turkey burned to a crisp, I poured three bowls of Cap'n Crunch, and a bit later we crawled into bed to go to sleep.

As I shared all this from the stage, I was intending to joke about it and tie it in with why Cap'n Crunch should be at the top of the food chain — but I found I couldn't speak. It was my habit to joke about things that were painful, but I stood there silent, unable to utter one word after sharing that memory. Thankfully, Bobby grabbed the microphone and covered for me, but I knew God was laying down the mandate that it was time to stop running. I needed to acknowledge my past instead of ignoring it or joking about it. I went home that night and got on my knees praying, "Lord, how do I deal with my past without getting stuck there? I want to love my parents, not blame them. I want to understand our lives, not rehash things that don't bring me closer to you."

It was during this reflective time that God made sense out of what I had run from. I was crushed by the weight of alcohol's destruction as I watched it turn my mom's beautiful face into a bulletin board pinned with despair. I was furious with my father who, the night of his car accident, had been caught with another woman and later rolled his car off the highway in a twisted smolder that left him paralyzed. Why alcohol? Why unfaithfulness, crippling our family and paralyzing more than my father's legs? These were the questions I finally had the courage to ask and the resolve to unravel.

After years of reflecting and begging God for understanding, my mom and I understood that she drank to keep from going crazy! Her mother shut down in a catatonic mental state of depression, and Mom knew she couldn't afford to do that. Alcohol served as a numbing agent, and when she was able to turn away from it, she did. For over thirty years she's been sober, and she has helped countless alcoholics find their way to freedom too.

That day on the stage was a watershed of awareness for me. I was finally ready to sort through my past without running or sinking. When I began to realize that the knots of my childhood were keeping me from growing as the Lord intended, I knew they had to go. I had pulled and yanked on some so tightly that only Jesus himself could give me the tools to loosen them. It was during this time that I learned the authentic method of awareness: acknowledge, accept, and anticipate.

Tools to Help Unravel the Past

When we're children, we don't always have the perspective to realize that adult screaming, raging, ignoring, and abusing are abnormal. But there comes a time when we need to *acknowledge* where we've come from — an awakening of sorts, an awareness that leads to growth.

My friend Annie was in her thirties when she began to struggle with an eating disorder. Interestingly, during this same time she also began to acknowledge the fact that she had been sexually abused by her dad while growing up. This was a secret she had buried deep within, encasing it with bubble wrap, hoping no one would make it pop. When she daringly began to unravel the abuse, the eating disorder lost its power and subsided. It was in the acknowledging of her pain that she was able to break free from it. This is where healing begins.

I was a late bloomer when it came to acknowledging. I kept beating myself up, wondering what was wrong with me, before I finally accepted the fact that my mom's struggle with alcohol and my dad's paralysis left imprints in the deepest crevices of my spirit. One day the principal of our elementary school, Sister Marilyn, pulled me and my siblings into her dark office for a chat. She bent down to eye level with the three of us as she said, "You kids are really going to have to try harder — especially you, Gari, since you're the oldest. You come to school and your hair isn't combed and your uniforms aren't ironed, and some days you don't have lunches packed."

I sorrowfully offered an apology, and promised we would try harder. It wasn't until I was an adult that I got mad about that conversation. Sister Marilyn knew our home life was chaotic, yet she was scolding us about combed hair, ironed uniforms, and packed lunches, when it was a miracle we got to school each day. Most days we walked several miles to get there, in all kinds of weather — who cares what our hair looked like when we arrived! Never once did anyone from that church help our family. Many years later, when I was able to acknowledge that things in my childhood were hard, I also began to accept that God used every year and event in my life to shape me into the woman I was meant to be. Even Sister Marilyn (whom I eventually respected and loved) played a part in the stitching of character that only God can sew in our lives.

To *accept* our past is to make peace with it — to quit pinching it, trying to get a reaction. Acceptance is where we learn empathy, both for ourselves and for the families we grew up in. The Bible describes empathy as compassion, and the psalms sing of its powerful balm.

> Praise the LORD, my soul,
>   and forget not all his benefits —
> who forgives all your sins
>   and heals all your diseases,
> who redeems your life from the pit
>   and crowns you with love and compassion,
> who satisfies your desires with good things
>   so that your youth is renewed like the eagle's.
>
>   PSALM 103:2 – 5

Compassion crowns us with a maturity that produces love, and love is the reflective image of our true parent, God. Sometimes it's tempting when we've come from a home of wounds to withhold compassion from those who wounded us. It's here that the balm of empathy soothes. Can you reflect on what made your parents, uncles, aunts, grandparents, and siblings act the way they did? Can you look objectively, without judgment, and accept the pain in their lives that caused them to inflict pain on you? Paul instructs us to put compassion on like a garment, like a piece of clothing that protects and covers our pain:

> Therefore, as God's chosen people, holy and dearly loved, clothe yourselves with compassion, kindness, humility, gentleness and patience. Bear with each other and forgive one another if any of you has a grievance against someone. Forgive as the Lord forgave you.
>
> COLOSSIANS 3:12 – 13

Notice that Paul doesn't add, "Go and be best friends," or, "Go and forget that anything ever happened." Many people get stuck on acceptance because they think it means negating the pain that was inflicted or placing themselves in harm's way if a parent or family member is better left alone. Paul is simply saying we should put this garment on so *we* can heal and move past what ties our heart in knots. Bitterness is a knot that must be unraveled. Someone else may have tied that knot on your rope, but forgiveness will untie it and untangle you.

Finally, we *anticipate*. This is where acknowledgment and acceptance cross the finish line in a satisfied blaze of glory. Our God is a God of anticipation; he is always reminding us of what we have to look forward to. If you've struggled with disappointment or pain from the way you were raised, you can joyfully anticipate that God has a life for you that is free from the confines of pain's definition. You can walk away joyously from the narrow chambers of your past to a spacious mansion built for your future. It doesn't matter how old you are; you are meant to live in a mansion of hope, not a shack of bitter regret.

Untying the knots of dysfunction in life brings the cloudy confusion of our pain into focus. It leads us to experience watershed moments where we see purpose in pain. Pastor Rick Warren writes:

There is nothing quite as potent as a focused life, one lived on purpose. The men and women who have made the greatest difference in history were the most focused. For instance, the apostle Paul almost single-handedly spread Christianity throughout the Roman Empire. His secret was a focused life. He said *"I am focusing all my energies on this one thing: Forgetting the past and looking forward to what lies ahead."*[5]

If we can shift our focus from what has been done to what is ahead — from the past to the promise of the future — we will experience a watershed of awareness that will expose and heal the blemished patches of our lives.

5

LOVE LIKE
A BEE STING

I've been stung by a bee three times in my life, and each time I was doing something that should have been fun — riding my bike, gathering fresh roses from my yard, and sitting at a ballgame on a Sunday afternoon. All were activities that should have brought a sigh of relaxation but ended with swatting, screaming, and swelling!

Sometimes love stings. Someone meant to cherish and protect ends up buzzing around with a stinger set on poke. And when that sting comes from a parent, it takes more than an icepack to relieve the swelling.

In the Bible, we are told that Abraham and Sarah's beloved son, Isaac, was finally ready for a bride, so Abraham sent a servant to Abraham's home country to find the right mate. When the servant laid eyes on Rebekah, the servant knew she was the one he had prayed for. She was a beautiful and gracious virgin, so he arranged for her to travel to Isaac's home and join him in marriage.

Always a lover of good romance, I can just picture the scene when Isaac first laid eyes on his betrothed. He was out in the fields praying when Rebekah rode onto the horizon, swaying gorgeously on her camel. From a distance they locked eyes, as the beginning of a tender love story began to unfold (Genesis 24).

It seems their first years of marriage were filled with joy and contentment, but slowly the pain of infertility would choke them, just as it choked Isaac's parents, Abraham and Sarah. Isaac prayed fervently that his wife would conceive, and after twenty years of prayer, Rebekah was finally "with child." Actually, much to their surprise, she was "with *children*" as she realized she was carrying twins.

The Bible tells us that these children "jostled each other within her" (Genesis 25:22). Her stomach was rolling from side to side with a fistfight between unborn brothers. Talk about pre-labor cramps. After praying to the Lord, she received this message:

> "Two nations are in your womb,
>   and two peoples from within you will be separated;
> one people will be stronger than the other;
>   and the older will serve the younger."
>
> GENESIS 25:23

How's that for a juicy birth announcement? From the womb these brothers were adversaries, and soon their parents would be adversaries too.

As the boys grew, the oldest son, Esau, became a skilled, meat-loving hunter — while Jacob was peaceful, spending most of his time in the tents with his mom. Within this family the table was set for one of the most damaging types of affection a parent can display — favoritism. "Isaac, who had a taste for wild game, loved Esau, but Rebekah loved Jacob" (Genesis 25:28).

In my opinion, favoritism is more damaging than neglect. Often neglect results from a parent's being overwhelmed with life's demands — job, finances, schedules. Favoritism chooses to willfully love one child more than another. Nothing hurts worse than trying to earn the affection of a parent who doesn't want to love you.

Playing favorites can usually be traced back to an initial event or characteristic that led a parent to turn up their nose at a child. Birth order, a child's appearance, behavioral patterns, or the child's lack of ability to learn or perform can contribute to an internal affection switch being shut down with a cold glance or harsh wag of the tongue.

When I was pregnant with my first child, I asked a mother of five how she kept from favoring one child over the other. She wisely responded, "I love each of my children equally, with a special dose of warmth for the one who needs me the most at the time."

I still refer to her wisdom today, as my adult children never seem to outgrow the need for encouragement or love from their mama. But let's be honest, the decades of diapers, sleepless nights, two-year-olds' tantrums, parent-teacher conferences, teenage meltdowns, and watching your beloved become independent provide plenty of opportunities to play favorites. If you have more than one child, the tension of children's different performances and behaviors buzzes through your home like a fly trying to land. As a young mom, I wrote this short prayer in my journal and vowed to live by its standards while raising my three lambs: *Lord, please help me to cultivate each of my children's strengths instead of comparing them or trying to squeeze them into the mold of another child. Amen.*

I've heard many conversations in which well-meaning moms shred their young with the swipe of an insensitive comment:

- You're so hard to love since you're not cuddly like your brother.
- You just don't get the grades your older sister does.
- Maybe if you looked as cute as your friends, you'd get asked out on dates.
- All the other kids in the class understood the directions; why didn't you?
- You need a lot of extra work in the batting cages if you want to hit the ball like the other kids on your team.
- Why can't you be a good girl like _____ ?

Sadly, these comments never motivate a child to change; they only feed favoritism's insatiable appetite. If left unchecked, the habit of selectively loving one child more than another can do more damage than almost any other parental flaw. Cultivating and building up rather than excavating and tearing down is the most powerful way a parent can cherish the bud of their child's personality that is struggling to bloom.

MY WAY OR THE HIGHWAY

Rebekah and Isaac's penchant toward favoritism was about to take a dangerous turn. When Rebekah overheard her husband tell their oldest son, Esau, to hunt some tasty meat for a meal at which he would give him the family blessing, she panicked as she thought about her favorite son, Jacob, missing out. In Eastern culture, the blessing was a big deal. Typically bestowed on the firstborn son, it meant he would get a double portion of the inheritance and become the leader of the family. This put Rebekah into full-blown manipulative mode as she concocted a plan to stop Esau's blessing.

> Now Rebekah was listening as Isaac spoke to his son Esau. When Esau left for the open country to hunt game and bring it back, Rebekah said to her son Jacob, "Look, I overheard your father say to your brother Esau, 'Bring me some game and prepare me some tasty food to eat, so that I may give you my blessing in the presence of the LORD before I die.' Now, my son, listen carefully and *do what I tell you*: Go out to the flock and bring me two choice young goats, so I can prepare some tasty food for your father, just the way he likes it. Then take it to your father to eat, so that he may give *you* his blessing before he dies."
>
> GENESIS 27:5 – 10, italics mine

Often when a parent says, "Do what I tell you!" it's because a child needs to quit arguing and do what they're being told to do. But in this case, Rebekah is waving her parental wand to conjure up a blessing of her own. She wants the blessing for her favorite boy because in some twisted way, it fills a need in her that hasn't been nurtured properly. Maybe it's the breakdown in her communication with Isaac (did you notice she was secretly listening to his conversation with Esau rather than participating in it?), or maybe she's had too much time on her hands in the tents. Either way, she's pushing for her needs to be met through her son's blessing.

In 1991, a woman named Wanda Holloway conjured up a bizarre plot to kill the mom of a rival young cheerleader so her daughter could make the squad. Her hope was that the rival cheerleader would be so devastated by her mother's death that she couldn't possibly try out for the cheerleading team, which would open up a spot for Wanda's daughter. Holloway's obsession seemed to stem from the fact that she had never been able to try out for cheerleader when she was young because of a strict upbringing.[6] This desire to satisfy her deep, unmet needs through the life of her child ended in a mess of knots that her unsuspecting daughter, Shanna, was left to unravel in the years to come. Although her mother's plot was thwarted before it could be executed, her mom went to prison, and Shanna endured years of torment as she tried to untie the knots that her mother had twisted and secured on her ropes.

Guiding children through their high school years taught me more lessons about my own insecurities than I care to admit. Each week I'd sit in the stands at a sporting event or in the audience at dance and cheer competitions, and find my normally low blood pressure rising to a boil. Moms and dads would scream, holler, and hoot, plotting their child's ascent to greatness or to the coveted college scholarship. Believe me, I hollered as loud as anyone, but often I'd feel overcome with an insecurity that I hadn't done enough to help my child succeed. Somehow it was my fault if my son or daughters weren't excelling. When they were performing well, I felt great, but if they were in a slump, injured, or not valued by a coach or teacher, I tried to think of ways to fix it — more pep talks, more private lessons, more hours examining why things weren't working out how I'd hoped they would. It didn't take long for me to crumble before God as I recognized *I* was trying to get a blessing. Somehow my kids' accomplishments were taking the place of my own affirmation and blessing from God.

One friend confided that she replaced her hollow longing for a husband with the love life of her teenage daughter. She lived out her desire for love through the crushes and heartaches of her teen, leaving both her and her daughter romantically exhausted. We're meant to live and thrive in our *own* lives — enjoying, celebrating, and encouraging our kids to become the men and women God has designed them to be. If we're pushy or needy, or if we find our moods rise and fall with our kids' performance, there's a good chance we're trying to get our blessing from a source other than God. And typically it's in the pursuit of counterfeit blessing that we become a bit bossy.

Rebekah is beginning to sound more like a nagging magpie than a loving mom, and her favored son is about to question her line of advice:

> Jacob said to Rebekah his mother, "But my brother Esau is a hairy man while I have smooth skin. What if my father touches me? I would appear to be tricking him and would bring down a curse on myself rather than a blessing."
>
> His mother said to him, "My son, let the curse fall on me. Just do what I say; go and get them [the goats] for me."
>
> GENESIS 27:11 – 13

It's interesting that Jacob doesn't want to deceive his father. This is something a parent should rejoice in! A child who runs from deception is a parent's dream come true. Isn't that what we spend years trying to build into a child?

Jacob senses this is a bad idea and tries to discourage his mom's advice, but it's "her way or the highway." She cares more about manipulating the circumstances than the heart of her child.

WHOSE DRAMA IS THIS?

If we could sit down for coffee with Rebekah, I promise she would say, "I only wanted what's best for my son." Who doesn't? I've never met a mother who openly states, "I want to ruin my child with my own unhealthy issues." But when we get down to the core of this problem, manipulative moms have a distorted view of themselves and their children, which eventually bleeds out over the family they seek to love.

What's really playing out here is a drama between Rebekah and her husband. Why isn't she talking to Isaac? Why aren't they presenting a united front in their love for God and their kids? Why aren't they spending more time together instead of so much time with their respective favorite children?

Recently Bobby and I asked our friends and acquaintances one simple question: "Do you love your kids more than you love your spouse?" Sadly, the answer was almost a unanimous yes. The consequences of this devastating revelation are far-reaching. When parents love their children more than their spouse, it places the child in an uncomfortable position of power. Often kids are sucked into triangulation, in which they become a type of child-counselor for an ailing adult.

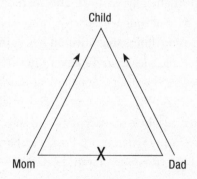

A year ago, I read about a celebrity mom who was strung out on prescription drugs and alcohol and was battling an eating disorder. Upon her admission to a treatment facility, her three daughters commented that they had been caring for her physically (making sure she ate and slept) and counseling her as she went through the breakup of her marriage. The kids had shouldered their mom's pain and the responsibility for her well-being, as well as counseling her and their stepfather through the process of their divorce. They were at the top of the triangle, trying to hold their family together in an unnatural way.

Last week my friend Taylor met me for iced tea in a quiet place where we love to talk. We've known each other for years and share a level of trust that respects the intricacies of unraveling knots. Sadly, she was placed at the top of a triangle, not by her mother and father, but by her mother and her mother's abusive boyfriend. This is how she described her pain:

"In 1980, I was nine years old. My parents had recently divorced, and I lived with my mother and younger brother. Soon after the divorce, Mom and Dad both moved on to other relationships. My dad's new wife didn't want much to do with my little brother and me. I desperately dreaded the 'every other weekend' exchanges because there always seemed to be a battle. I walked on eggshells most of the time. I did my time at my dad's house but never really felt welcome in his home.

"My mother had been dating a man fifteen years her senior. He was successful and financially well-off, and by the time I was eleven he began spending a lot of time with us. My mother was a hard worker and dealt with a chronic illness that affected her vulnerable emotional state, but she was hard to please, and I never knew what kind of mood she'd be in. We moved around a lot, which meant new schools and new classes. I began to struggle in school and soon was labeled with a form of dyslexia to add to my labels of insecurity and self-doubt. I turned to sports as an outlet for my frustration. Basketball and softball helped me keep my grades up enough to play and gave me a set of new friends when I'd find myself at another new school.

"By the time I turned eleven, my mom's boyfriend began paying a lot of attention to me. It wasn't long before his attention turned to sexual abuse. One afternoon I returned home on the school bus to find my grandparents sitting in our living room. Although I was only a sixth grader, I knew something was terribly wrong. My grandmother told me Mom had been locked in her room all day with a gun, threatening to take her life after suspecting her boyfriend was cheating on her. I was terrified to realize he was cheating on her with me! Grandma warned me to be a good girl and not cause any problems for my mom.

"We continued to move, mostly to go into hiding after violent break-ups between my mom and her boyfriend. It was a nice reprieve from the abuse, but moving wasn't easy. I was always the new girl — so I began inventing who I wanted to be. When girls would talk about boys, I would pretend to be as naive as they were. One day at lunch, I grabbed my tray of cafeteria food and began to scan the tables to see where I might fit in. My knees nearly buckled as I looked out over the groups of girls sitting in their comfortable places. Where would I sit? Who would I be? I took my food to the bathroom and ate it behind the closed door of a stall.

"Graduation couldn't come soon enough, but the scars of my past seemed to follow me into my future as I married the first guy to come along. He was physically, verbally, and emotionally abusive, and I ended up divorced at the age of twenty-one. One of the few things my parents did right before they divorced was occasionally take me to church. At age six I was baptized, and I often prayed to Jesus and sang songs to him in delight. But it didn't take long for me to question where he had gone. How did I end up in such a mess?

"On Easter Sunday, thirteen years after my parents' divorce and the span of years that sought to destroy me, I experienced a watershed of awareness. I knew my life was moving toward ruin, and I felt drawn to cry out to the God I remembered from when I was a young girl. I walked into a church, and the Lord met me there. A fire was ignited in my soul that gave me great hope. I began to read my Bible and listen to teaching tapes and Christian music. I sought work in the entertainment business, working on commercials, hosting shows, and serving as the promotions director for a Christian show. Over time, even my mom rededicated her life to Christ and began a healing passage of promise and hope.

"God has unraveled and restored my life in ways that only a Savior can. I'm now married to a pastor, have two beautiful kids, and live each day with the realization that my past does not dictate my future. Only God does, and that's a watershed splashed in glory."

HEALTHY TRIANGLES

A healthy triangle has God at its point, with both parents confiding in him and each other. The child can then thrive in the center, benefiting from the communication between parents and God. Even in families of divorce, if Mom and Dad are civilly talking to God and one another, the child has the rightful place of importance in the center of the triangle.

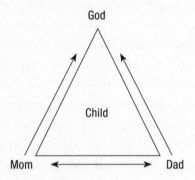

For those of us whose childhood triangles may have looked more like a lopsided rhombus, rest assured, it doesn't matter what shape your life has taken; God can straighten it out.

Because of the horrendous position my mom found herself in after my dad's car accident, our triangle morphed into a squiggly line. God was a distant question mark; her husband (my dad) was silent and depressed; her new normal revolved around the threat of bedsores, brain damage, and wheelchair ramps. As the oldest, I assumed the role of care-taker for my younger siblings and as a sounding board for my mom and grandparents. I learned which dance to dance with whom, trying not to step on toes and cause the family pain. This approach worked when I was young, but as I matured I became rebellious and resentful. My rebellion didn't leak out in the form of drinking or wild behavior. As a matter of fact, I steered clear of drinking and was terrified of being wild! Instead, my rebellion played out in the form of self-hatred and insecurity. I rebelled against any love I was shown, feeling sure that anyone trying to give love would be sadly disappointed by wasting it on me. I resented the need to cover for alcoholism and to excuse the absurdity of a family that teetered on the brink of calamity. Thankfully, the threat of calamity eventually gave way to the cloak of surrender, as both of my parents made their peace with God, one another, and their children.

But what happens when a parent refuses to surrender? What if the push to be in charge outweighs the pull for peace and sanity?

OPEN REBELLION OR QUIET PASSIVITY?

After Rebekah coerced Jacob into tricking his father for the blessing, Jacob's older brother, Esau, came undone when he discovered that his blessing had been stolen. He wasn't the only one who was upset. His father, Isaac, "trembled violently" when he learned he had been tricked (Genesis 27:33). Esau, a hairy huntsman, crumbled in tears as he cried out, "Bless me — me too, my father!" (Genesis 27:34). You can almost see the quiver of his lips as he begs his father to retract the blessing. But Isaac affirms that the blessing can't be revoked. What's done is done, which sends Esau into a state of blistering revenge.

Here's where Rebekah could have had a watershed moment. She could have acknowledged her deceitful influence and alleviated the murderous tension between her boys. Instead, she chose to duck and cover. When she heard of her older son's plot to murder, she recoiled in self-protection as she spoke to her beloved Jacob.

> When Rebekah was told what her older son Esau had said, she sent for her younger son Jacob and said to him, "Your brother Esau is planning to avenge himself by killing you. Now then, my son, do what I say: Flee at once to my brother Laban in Harran. Stay with him for a while until your brother's fury subsides. When your brother is no longer angry with you and forgets what *you* did to him, I'll send word for you to come back from there. Why should I lose both of you in one day?"
>
> GENESIS 27:42 – 45, italics mine

The nerve of this mother! She was the one who concocted the devious plan that shattered her entire family, and then she blames Jacob for how it turned out! Sadly, manipulative moms cause children to become either openly rebellious or quietly passive. Both reactions rip through the fabric of a family swifter than a pair of sharp scissors cuts through paper.

Esau openly rebelled with a threat of murder. Rebekah knew that if Esau murdered his brother, he would then be killed according to the law. Again her selfish nature flares when she moans to Jacob that she can't bear to lose *both* of her sons — because, you know, it's all about her. Jacob remains quietly passive, doing as Mommy says, but stuffing away his manhood and beliefs, passively accepting her reign. From this time forth, both of her sons left her — Esau clinging to his father while offering the cold shoulder toward a mother who never fully loved him, and Jacob fleeing from his mother's claws and his twin brother's fiery threats.

DADDY DRAMA

Jacob did as he was told and made his way to his uncle Laban's home. It didn't take long to see that his uncle was a lot like his mom, prone to favoritism and crafty maneuvers. Laban had two daughters who were as different as Jacob and his brother, Esau, were.

> Now Laban had two daughters; the name of the older was Leah, and the name of the younger was Rachel. Leah had weak eyes, but Rachel had a lovely figure and was beautiful.
>
> GENESIS 29:16 – 17

Right here we have a problem. Imagine being described as a daughter with coke-bottle glasses instead of a daughter with a stunning face and figure. It's hard enough to navigate the waters of growing up, never mind the heartache of not looking as good as your sister. In our society, as in that one, how we look often determines how we feel about ourselves.

As I stood in the grocery store line waiting to check out, my eyes grazed magazine headlines that screamed at me louder than fireworks:

- Erase the lines of your age and look younger in ten days.
- Carve the plump out of your belly with our fat-burning supplement.
- Makeup that changes the flaws you hate!
- Perfect hair, perfect skin, perfect teeth — perfect 10!

No wonder we're confused. If physical perfection were as easy as these headlines promise, we'd all look like supermodels. But here's a secret: I've known many models, and *they* don't even look like the pictures taken of them. Their skin still breaks out; they have days they can't zip their jeans; and they worry they aren't as pretty as the new girl who waltzes onto the stage of their lives.

Rachel and Leah were raised by a dad bent on using his girls for his maximum benefit. Parents who care more about themselves than their children have a way of doing this, and these sisters were about to muck around in the residue of their dad's selfishness. Parents like Laban expect their children to take out their trash — rancid and reeking with an awful stench — and Rachel and Leah aren't the only ones struggling with trash. After working for years to win the hand of Rachel in marriage, Jacob found himself still functioning in passivity — the same passivity he had adopted as a coping strategy during his youth. All three of these adult children were trying to figure out their own waste management and how to end up anywhere but in their parents' dump!

Seven years of servitude eventually passed as Jacob's highly anticipated wedding night finally arrived. Filled with excitement, Jacob must have had too much to drink because his eyesight and senses were impaired. Tricky Laban switched his daughters on Jacob's marriage bed, replacing Rachel with weak-eyed Leah. For the life of me, I can't figure out why Jacob didn't notice this, but it wasn't until morning that he stormed into Laban's tent and raised his voice. Passive Jacob finally got mad!

His uncle promised that at the end of Jacob's bridal week with Leah, he could have his beloved Rachel as a wife. But it was going to take another seven years of work to make it legal. Laban married off both his daughters and got free labor for fourteen years — not bad for a conniving man. But putting two sisters in a marriage with the same man is like putting two pit bulls in a cage and yelling, "Lie down!" Blood will be drawn, and sadly this blood came from the crying hearts of both sisters.

STICKS AND STONES

Imagine being in love with a man who spends one night with you in your tent and several with your sister in her tent. Each week, these sisters vied for the attention of their husband. Leah began having babies, and that helped her feel better about her sour looks — for a while. Rachel struggled to get pregnant, and although she was physically stunning and loved by her husband, try as they might, she couldn't have children. The plot is as thick as a milkshake, and no amount of whipped cream can sweeten the pain these girls felt as they watched their hopes for love, family, and motherhood melt around them.

Sometimes I wonder if their dad, Laban, even noticed the pain he was causing. His selfish motive to marry off his oldest daughter when he knew Jacob loved his younger daughter started a domino run of destruction. He cared more about tradition and personal gain, and about how his family looked to outsiders, than about the hearts of his own girls. If he had protected them or even been honest with Jacob about the traditions he felt bound to, he might have experienced a watershed moment, and the jealousy, competition, and anxiety might have been avoided.

Over the years, I've collected some of the comments I've heard from women as they reflect on words spoken to them by their dads:

- My dad told me if I ever wanted a man to love me, I needed to lose ten to twenty-five pounds.
- My dad repeatedly announced I wasn't smart enough to have a career so I better learn how to serve drinks and wait on tables.
- My dad basically ignored me until I was a teenager, and when I became a teen, he daily whispered comments that made me feel terrified of men.
- My dad said that pretty girls get men's attention, and since I wasn't pretty I better learn to be funny or to be a good housekeeper.
- My dad took my sister and me for breast implants on our sixteenth birthdays.

Each of these comments is devastating, but the last one leaves me shaking my head. Imagine the implications for a teenager when, at age sixteen, it's Daddy who says it's time to change your body! Thankfully, this story has a beautiful outcome, as the sixteen-year-old girl became a woman who loved Jesus. She shared with her friends that she didn't feel good about the body Daddy insisted on, and after prayerful consideration, she decided to have the breast implants removed. That day she felt a freedom and release from the damaging motives of a reckless father.

Although my father was distant and quiet after his car accident, it wasn't until I was a grown woman that I realized how much I longed for my dad's love. One day a little note arrived in the mail. The return address had my father's name in the corner, and since it was extremely hard for him to write, I anxiously opened the letter. The note had large flowers in fall colors — reds, oranges, and golds — laced along its side. At the top, a greeting was embossed on the paper in bold letters: **A Note from Gary**. Instinctively I knew this note was a big deal, because in order for my dad to write, he had to strap an arm brace on with his teeth and roll a pen several times before finding just the right angle to pick it up. As tears slid down my face, I read the words I knew he had labored to express.

Dear Gari,

A note to tell you how much I love you. Last year after my kidney surgery it really struck me how much you, your sister, and your brother mean to me. I'm so proud of you. You and Bobby are raising a great family.

Love,
Dad

It wasn't long or drawn out. It didn't have gorgeous language or cadence, but it was from my dad, and that's what mattered. I don't have many mementos from him; as a matter of fact, I hardly have any pictures or ways to recall the man who loved me in his quiet way. But I have his note tucked in the corner of my Bible, and this note marked a watershed moment.

That day as I fell to the kitchen floor with his note in my trembling hand, I made peace with my parents. All the terrifying days and disappointing nights, the bitterness and regret, seemed to wash away as a watershed of awareness laid bare my knots. I no longer felt the need to look at my knots in frustration or to pull on them in an attempt to make them go away. God made sense of the knots and unraveled them for me, leaving a smooth rope of compassion and purpose from the knotted fray of the fibers of the past.

Awareness is light that gives way to truth. If we allow the light of awareness to shine over pain, a new purpose will emerge. As the apostle Paul puts it, "Forgetting what is behind and straining toward what is ahead, I press on toward the goal to win the prize for which God has called me heavenward in Christ Jesus" (Philippians 3:13 – 14).

Part Three

THE
WATERSHED OF
REBUILDING

6

VISIONARIES

When I was three years old, my vision went haywire. After a bout with the measles, my eyesight was drastically altered, and suddenly I was the proud owner of a light blue pair of cat-eyed glasses.

Trying to get a three-year-old to wear glasses is a bit like telling a turkey to sit. In my case, it would have been more believable to see a gobbler resting in a chair than to see me wearing those glasses. My mom tells stories of finding them in the strangest places. One time I even dropped them into the gas tank of our car!

My parents had begged me for months to keep the corrective glasses on my face, when a stroke of luck came my way. The cat-eyed glasses broke right down the middle. (I wonder if I had anything to do with that!) After a trip to the eye doctor, he proclaimed I was healed, and I boasted perfect vision from that day forward. Somehow in my shoddy commitment to wearing those glasses, my vision was restored — much to the relief of my weary mom.

I've often wondered if God doesn't build spiritual vision much like he corrected the altered vision of my youth. Before we recognize God, we run around hiding his insight in gas tanks of confusion or self-centered assurance. But when our eyes have been healed, we're able to see more clearly. The apostle Paul was struck blind for three days before he could see, and once he "saw" Jesus in the dark, there was no stopping the vision Paul carried into the light.

The great writer Oswald Chambers writes, "The vision Paul had on the road to Damascus was no passing emotion, but a vision that had very clear and emphatic directions for him ... When we are born again we all have visions, if we are spiritual at all, of what Jesus wants us to be, and the great thing is to learn not to be disobedient to the vision, not to say that it cannot be attained."[7]

The problem is that we tend to confuse *dreams* with *vision*. For our purposes, we need to put some fences around these words. Dreams may or may not be stitched in reality. They may be a fun mental escape from the drudgery of the mundane, or the hope of overcoming the dead-end cycles we find ourselves living in daily.

All of us can think back to things we dreamed of when we were young. I dreamed of being a singer, and so I stood in front of a mirror with a brush microphone in my hand, hoping that someday I'd supernaturally receive a good voice. I dreamed of being a movie star, and so I walked around my room in high heels and a boa, pretending to be famous. I dreamed of making the basketball team, but after struggling to dribble in tryouts, I spent years cheering from the sidelines.

As I grew older, some of my dreams became tangible. I dreamed of making a difference, so I taught school. I dreamed of being a writer, so I wrote for any publication that would give me a free byline. But some of my dreams weren't as noble: a flat stomach, a cottage on the beach, kids who earned perfect grades. There's nothing wrong with dreams; as a matter of fact, it's healthy to have dreams that inspire hope. But there's a difference between the casual flitting of a dream and the weighty purpose of a vision.

A vision is God-centered and God-ordained. Visions extend across time; they're not immediately delivered but rather gain momentum through obedience and prayer. Pastor and author Andy Stanley writes, "Visions are born in the soul of a man or woman who is consumed with the tension between what is and what could be ... Anyone with a vision will tell you this is not merely something that *could* be done. This is something that *should* be done."[8]

Visions aren't cloaked in a mystic veil. Typically they're conveyed when a watershed moment swells to a mandate toward action: We must move. We must hope. We must build.

The notion of vision and building are linked in God's Word. When God gives his people a glimpse of possibility, the steady hope of building on a vision takes us from yearning to certainty. Most people understand the process of building — the actual brick-by-brick labor that gets things done. But *vision* can be a bit blurry.

The first time I built on a vision given to me by God, it came with a physical price tag. I was sickened by my body as I muddled through the mental fog of disordered eating. Some months were filled with uncontrollable binges and the self-hatred I wallowed in after eating recklessly. Other months I'd starve and exchange one compulsion for another. I knew I had to either change or live as a hypocrite. How could I teach that with Jesus you can know the truth that will set you free, and yet continue to live in the chains of slavery to food and self-image? My faith and my actions needed to match, and this is where I dared to respond to the vision God was birthing within me. God and I had some "hashing it out" sessions as I wrote out a vision I knew was being embossed in my spirit regarding the disconnect I had with my body.

I wanted to live in a body I was proud of; I wanted to be healthy, trim, and most of all, free from compulsion with food. This seemed about as possible as rowing a boat to China, but I began to pray about how God would merge this vision with action in my life. I studied, I wrote, and I obeyed as I prayed for a good "life weight" for me — not what I weighed when I was twelve but rather a weight I could maintain for the rest of my life. The next thing I did was immerse myself in the truth of God's Word. Surprisingly, God has a lot to say about our habits with food, and I took what he said seriously. The vision was set — freedom, healing, and eventually the ability to help others out of the pantry I had been locked in for too long.

My first published book is titled *Truly Fed: Finding Freedom from Disordered Eating*, and every time I see this book, I think of the vision

God and I brought to fruition. To this day, I still live by the principles he led me to unpack in that book, and twenty-six years later, I still weigh the weight I prayed about when crafting that vision! Remember, visions don't magically happen; they have to be built, and building something takes deliberate and intentional effort.

Another vision I participated in involved the desire I had to speak and write about God. I had read my first Christian nonfiction book while flying home from a visit to see Bobby the first season he played pro baseball. A precocious twenty-one-year-old, I sat on that plane with tears filling my little cup of Coke. Each page beckoned me, enticing me to splash my love for a Savior on the ocean of a page. I begged God to take me to the pulpit of publishing, and I laid out my commitment to moving forward. It was deliberate and intentional, with prayer and steps of obedience that pushed me past my fears.

It was twenty years before I formally got a book published, but during that time I wrote continuously. I wrote for a Christian sports magazine; I had a column in a small magazine and newspaper; I contributed to book projects within the confines of education — and most importantly, for seventeen years I taught third graders to write. It wasn't enough for them to merely write; I wanted them to love it — to crave it — like I did. The first page of our writing journals held this quote from the Mexican novelist Carlos Fuentes: "Language permits us to see. Without words, we are blind." We didn't just write words; we harvested them to nourish our prose.

My writing and speaking platform grew from small retreats and gatherings, Christmas talks, and living room Bible studies to teaching close to a thousand women each week at my home church in Houston. That in itself was the fruit of a vision bestowed on the women's director at our church and me. Before we ever promoted a gathering, we huddled in prayer on a crusty couch that sat in a storage room of furniture. We would pray and weep as God gave us vision regarding the fresh breath he wanted to blow across his women. After the vision, we had to be faithful to execute what he revealed on that dirty orange couch. Some steps were simple, while others were so overwhelming we could only roll our desire back onto the spine of God and see how he would manage the weight of our anticipation.

I guess I'm a slow learner because it doesn't have to take decades to see a vision bear fruit. But the glory of a vision is seeing how God uses every brick to build the walls we pray for.

Who sees with the eyes of such vision? What kind of man or woman thinks like this? You may be surprised to find they're all around us. My friends Lori Ann and Scott have prayed to produce a movie that seems impossible to make. They have faithfully endured years of meetings, hope, and setbacks as they continue to lay their vision before God and add bricks where he instructs. Pastor Mark Batterson talks about his desire to start a church on Washington, DC's, Capitol Hill. What started as a whisper and a vision is now a multisite powerhouse of faith in Washington, DC. My friend Alisha has turned down several chances to marry as she waits for her vision of the man she feels is her God-given soul mate. My worship leader, Rhonda, followed her vision to produce a CD despite her fears and surgery on her vocal cords. And Andrea and Leah, two sisters from Colorado, started an orphanage in Uganda when they were both in their twenties and broke!

Visionaries are those who dare to put their desire on the line. They're willing to take talk and give it legs, to take prayer and help it fly. People who act on visions have learned a critical perspective: They've learned how to work within a crisis. Sometimes that crisis is one of emotion. "I can't do this! It's too big and consuming." Sometimes the crisis comes in the form of circumstantial problems and blockades. I once heard a pastor say, "Problems are opportunities in disguise." When everyone else is wringing their hands in worry and defeat, God wants us to be the ones who believe he can take our God-centered vision and continue to forge ahead.

Visions don't just address what we hope to do for God's glory; they also address who we hope to become. A God-given vision isn't dependent on how we see ourselves; it's fueled by how God sees *us*.

God called Gideon "mighty warrior" long before he went to battle (Judges 6:12). He called Mary "you who are highly favored" before she was pregnant (Luke 1:28). Both of these unlikely believers would be transformed by the vision God invited them to join. When we heed God's invitation, we respond to him in such a way that we not only act differently for his glory but also become something different within his glory.

The beauty of a vision is that we can cast them for those we love, as well as for those God brings into our lives who may need someone to see them not as they are but as they could be. Andy Stanley writes, "The most significant visions are not cast by great orators from a stage. They are cast at the bedsides of our children."[9] What would happen if generations of parents, teachers, coaches, and mentors cast vision for the children around them, speaking to the future, hope, and promise of all that God can muster in their lives? What if we built into their hearts what the world tries to leak out?

Andy's father is the well-known preacher Charles Stanley. Andy shares how at an early age, he remembers his daddy saying, "Andy, God has something very special for your life. He is going to use you in a great way." During Andy's tentative years in high school, he experienced a watershed moment as his father's words echoed in his mind, protecting him from choices that may have led him away from his father's vision. The fall of his senior year Andy wrote this in his journal:

> September 29, 1975
> I need to tell my boy at a young age that God told me he was going to use my son in a great way. This greatly influenced my life. Lord, I pray it will his.[10]

At the tender age of eighteen, Andy was already casting vision for the son he didn't yet have. His father's repeated vision made the difference in Andy's life, and the deliberate parental moves his father made while guiding Andy through his childhood were built around this vision. Vision casting isn't the chance to shove on someone an agenda that isn't God-ordained; it's merely the opportunity to believe that God can build something worthy if we have the eyes to see it and participate in it.

A Faithful Visionary's Birth of a Vision

The Bible shows a stunning example of a visionary in Nehemiah. A God-fearing Jew, Nehemiah lived through his share of heartache. His homeland of Jerusalem was pillaged and captured, not once, but three times, with many of his fellow citizens led into captivity. After one of these invasions, the Jews were allowed to go back and rebuild the temple that had been destroyed, but after the initial thrill had worn off, sacrifices ceased and the temple fell into disrepair. The Jews adopted the culture and practices of those around them, and the wall that originally protected this great city of God-fearing people crumbled and was filled with holes — a true representation of their spiritual life.

Nehemiah was living in Persia, serving as cupbearer to King Artaxerxes, the son of the king who had married Esther. Maybe that's what made Nehemiah such a good listener. During a visit from Nehemiah's brother Hanani and some other friends from Judah, Nehemiah asked about the Jews who had survived the captivity and about the condition of his beloved Jerusalem. The answer he received pierced him in an inexplicable way: "Those who survived the exile and are back in the province are in great trouble and disgrace. The wall of Jerusalem is broken down, and its gates have been burned with fire" (Nehemiah 1:3).

Nehemiah knew what this meant. His Jewish brothers and sisters were being teased, mocked, and made fun of. They were a reproach to all who looked on them. And if that weren't enough, the iconic wall that enclosed the city had been torn down.

Walls mean little to us today, but in Nehemiah's day they were essential: "They offered safety from raids and symbolized strength and peace."[11] Although he lived his entire life in Babylon, Nehemiah knew his homeland was desperate — desperate for hope and desperate for vision. From this achy place of desperation, Nehemiah hit a turning point — a watershed moment sparking passion and emotion.

When Nehemiah heard about the crumbled wall, he did the manliest thing he could have done — he sat down and cried. In fact, he cried for days, and he refused to eat. Nothing could jar him out of this prayerful stance as he experienced the birth of a God-centered vision.

Within the gestation of his vision, he did nothing but pray. That's it — just pray. Sometimes it's tempting to think that "just pray" is a weak effort that leads to the complacency of doing nothing. But when a vision is being infused in a believer, prayer is the most essential component. Without it we're using our own strength and common sense as a compass, and I know my common sense could lead a pack of women off a cliff. Even with all our books and commentaries, we still understand so little about the power of prayer.

One day as I was praying, I asked God to show me what our prayers look like to him. Remarkably, he showed me something that left me speechless. In the book of Revelation, John describes a scene in which the Lamb — Jesus — takes a scroll in his hands. John writes, "And when he had taken it, the four living creatures and the twenty-four elders fell down before the Lamb. Each one had a harp and they were holding golden bowls full of incense, which are the prayers of God's people" (Revelation 5:8). John later explains where these prayers end up: "The smoke of the incense, together with the prayers of God's people, went up before God from the angel's hand" (Revelation 8:4).

When was the last time you felt assured your prayers were filling the nostrils of God? So often we wander around wondering if God even hears us when, truthfully, he is inhaling the scent of every word we utter. He not only hears; he listens, assures, weeps, feels, and accepts every kind of prayer we articulate, both with our mouths and with our hearts. Our prayers gather in golden bowls that move directly into God's presence. Praying is the most effective thing we'll ever do.

Nehemiah hunkered down in prayer for four months before he ever shared his vision with a soul. The Bible says he began praying in the month of Kislev (December) and then made his first move in the month of Nisan (April). During these prayerful months, Nehemiah positioned himself in a prayer posture worth noting:

Nehemiah confessed. He spent the first part of this prayer progression pouring his sorrow out to God.

> "O Lord God," I cried out; "O great and awesome God who keeps his promises and is so loving and kind to those who love and obey him! Hear my prayer! Listen carefully to what I say! Look down and see me praying night and day for your people Israel. I confess that we have sinned against you; yes, I and my people have committed the horrible sin of not obeying the commandments you gave us through your servant Moses."
>
> NEHEMIAH 1:5 – 7 LB

Nehemiah lumps himself right in the middle of Jews he doesn't know firsthand but has a spiritual kinship with. He doesn't say, "Forgive all those people of my faith who have sinned"; he says, "*We* have sinned; forgive *us!*" If we ever want to be part of a God-centered vision, we must identify with those we want to help. When it comes to sin, it's something we're all responsible for.

Nehemiah reminds God of his promises. He doesn't do this in a rude way like a child trying to manipulate a parent. He does it with the utmost respect.

> "Oh, please remember what you told Moses! You said,
>   *'If you sin, I will scatter you among the nations; but if you return to me and obey my laws, even though you are exiled to the farthest corners of the universe, I will bring you back to Jerusalem. For Jerusalem is the place in which I have chosen to live.'"*
>
> NEHEMIAH 1:8 – 9 LB

With confidence in the way in which God spoke to his ancestors, Nehemiah reiterates what God already has mandated.

Nehemiah asks God for favor and success. This next petition proves that Nehemiah is ready to act on his vision.

> "We are your servants, the people you rescued by your great power. O Lord, please hear my prayer! Heed the prayers of those of us who delight to honor you. Please help me now as I go in and ask the king for a great favor — put it into his heart to be kind to me."
>
> NEHEMIAH 1:10 – 11 LB

His predicament reminds me a bit of what the king's mother, Esther, must have experienced before she asked her husband for a favor. It's really God who moves the mountains that stand in the way of our vision, and he teaches us to climb the ones he allows to remain.

FROM PRAYER TO ACTION

After an intense and focused period of prayer, Nehemiah is ready to act. He brought the king's wine to him, as he normally did, but the king sensed there was nothing normal about the sad look on Nehemiah's face.

> In the month of Nisan in the twentieth year of King Artaxerxes, when wine was brought for him, I took the wine and gave it to the king. I had not been sad in his presence before, so the king asked me, "Why does your face look so sad when you are not ill? This can be nothing but sadness of heart."
>
> I was very much afraid, but I said to the king, "May the king live forever! Why should my face not look sad when the city where my ancestors are buried lies in ruins, and its gates have been destroyed by fire?"
>
> The king said to me, "What is it you want?"
>
> Then I prayed to the God of heaven, and I answered the king,

"If it pleases the king and if your servant has found favor in his
sight, let him send me to the city in Judah where my ancestors are
buried so that I can rebuild it."

NEHEMIAH 2:1 – 5

I love Nehemiah's raw honesty. He came right out and said, "I was
very much afraid." Many times in my life I've been "very much afraid"
and covered it by eating, sleeping, ignoring, or pretending. There's
something refreshing about a man who is not embarrassed to say, "I'm
scared." Nehemiah chose maturity over macho when he poured out
his pain before the king rather than cowering in a corner, whimper-
ing, "Everything's fine." Nehemiah didn't know it, but he was about to
experience another watershed moment, a moment he had prayed for
and sheltered in his vision.

When the king asked, "What do you need?" it was as if he was saying, "Yes, and how can I help?" Nehemiah knew this was his moment,
and he was prepared. After four months of prayer and vision crafting,
he knew exactly how to respond. It didn't mean he wasn't still scared,
because before he could even articulate a response, he prayed.

Sometimes we pray like a Crock-Pot — slow, steady, and complete.
Other times we pray like a microwave — quick to hear the ding of a
timer because we need our help fast. Like the inhale of a breath, this
prayer was brief but essential because Nehemiah had a captive audience for the vision that was transforming his heart — and the watershed moment that would transform a nation.

Nehemiah wisely gave definitive answers when the king asked
for specifics. He didn't hem and haw, backpedal, or say, "Well, whatever you think is OK." He came right out with it, and because he had
a God-centered vision, he was able to answer the king. He knew he
needed timber to use for construction, so he asked that a letter be
given to the keeper of the forest allowing Nehemiah access to the
wood. He knew the time frame for his work, so he explained that to
the king as well. With full support, the king sent army officers and
the cavalry with Nehemiah as he delivered his letters to the governors

of the surrounding areas, explaining that he was going to rebuild the broken wall of Jerusalem.

But now we see the unyielding reality of any vision we try to engage: there will be opposition, and the opposition is pesky.

WAKING UP YOUR ADVERSARIES

When the Japanese were en route over the Pacific to bomb Pearl Harbor, a Japanese naval commander proclaimed to the chief officer of the fleet that Japan would soon be the greatest world power, eliminating the superpower status of the United States. The chief commander looked reflectively at his comrade and said, "I fear all we have done is to awaken a sleeping giant and fill him with a terrible resolve."[12]

Jerusalem had once been a great city containing a formidable people with a formidable faith in God. Now these people were a laughingstock. None of the surrounding territories took them seriously; the Jews didn't even take *themselves* seriously. But as soon as Nehemiah began to believe that things could be different, a sleeping giant awoke.

After living in a spiritual slumber for decades, the Jews were about to do something great. They were about to rebuild more than a wall; they would rebuild their faith and commitment to God, and Nehemiah was going to show them how.

But here's where things get tricky. Whenever we move past complacency toward the hope that inhabits a vision, we're not the only sleeping giant that awakes. Our adversaries awake too — the pesky, annoying, and sometimes debilitating forces that try to obliterate our vision and tie our hands behind our backs. In Nehemiah's case, his adversaries had names: "When Sanballat the Horonite and Tobiah the Ammonite official heard about this, they were very much disturbed that someone had come to promote the welfare of the Israelites" (Nehemiah 2:10).

Not everyone was happy that the mild-mannered Jews would rebuild their wall. Sanballat and Tobiah were politicians, and this political move infuriated them. They liked things the way they were and didn't want anyone stirring up the hope and faith of a people who once were strong. These men proved to be the worst kind of adversaries — the kind best described as "Satan in a suit." These were the men Satan pushed like puppets to discourage Nehemiah any way they could.

I wish we could hear the conversation Satan has with his posse of demons whenever a believer gets serious about their love for God. It might go something like this: *"Oh shoot, she knows that Jesus is real and truly loves her. Oh no! She's starting to talk about this love to other people. Ahhhh! She's not afraid anymore, and she's helping other people understand the truth! We need to distract her or lie to her or something!"*

When was the last time *you* scared Satan? It seems we spend so much time playing defense that we forget that believers are on the offense. God is calling the shots through us, his receptive people. We are participating in the plays that bring victory to God.

Years ago, I adopted a phrase that helps me put this perspective in place. After fighting and flailing when I saw Satan's attempts to paralyze my growth, I realized that Satan wasn't going anywhere — but I didn't have to allow him to walk around with me. I started to discipline him like I would an unruly child. I began to say, "Go sit on the couch!" to this nagging pest.

To this day, if he tries to speak to me, I say, "Sit on the couch! You aren't allowed to follow me throughout my day." Jesus simply said, "Get behind me, Satan!" (Matthew 16:23). Notice he didn't engage him in a long dialogue of religious mumbo jumbo; he simply said, "Go away," and that was enough to put Satan in his place.

Sometimes it's hard to know exactly what or who your adversaries are. They can look hazy at times. Is there someone who bullies you? Someone who torments you verbally, physically, or sexually? Someone who comes against you because of their own jealousy or insecurity? Someone who threatens you or pins you down in guilt, deceit, or manipulation? These are adversaries seeking to harm your spirit. They long to hold you in place and punch you until you give up.

Other times, our adversaries may look like discouragement, distraction, fear, self-pity, self-hatred, or the overwhelming feeling that who you are doesn't matter. These are murmuring adversaries that must be told to sit. We may be looking back at that couch with tears, bruised and battered but not defeated. If we have the guts to make them flee, they have to go.

David spoke to God about his adversaries with desperate confidence. He knew that God alone could turn them back.

> Away from me, all you who do evil,
>   for the LORD has heard my weeping.
> The LORD has heard my cry for mercy;
>   the LORD accepts my prayer.
> All my enemies will be overwhelmed with shame and anguish;
>   they will turn back and suddenly be put to shame.
>
> PSALM 6:8 – 10

Your adversaries, whoever they are or whatever they look like, will turn back and suddenly be put to shame. What a comfort to know that *we* aren't put to shame; our adversaries are! We need to remember this truth when we're feeling the heat of their breath and hearing the rasp of their voice.

Never have I felt the heat of my adversaries as blatantly as I did a few months ago when I took a team of women to Uganda. This trip challenged me so profoundly — physically and spiritually — that I felt like I had an army of adversaries sitting on a couch behind me.

Every piece of clothing was tucked in place. My shredded Adidas suitcase was the perfect choice for a trip I knew would make the word *rugged* look tame. I tried to prepare my team of eight women for the experiences that lay ahead. We were traveling to Uganda to work at an orphanage and then heading to the northern territory where I had been asked to speak at a conference called the "Miracle Crusade." In one of our planning sessions, a sweet team member asked, "Will the hotel rooms have a safe?" I laughed as I explained they may not have running water or electricity!

On the day we left for the airport, the rain was pouring down, which made loading the car a bit tricky. It wasn't until we got to the airport that I realized my backpack, which housed my passport and money, was still sitting on my front porch. The most important thing on my mind was getting my team on that flight. It's a two-day journey to Uganda, so with the assurance that I'd join them a day late, I uttered these fateful words to a member of my team who was crying at the ticket counter. "If this is the best Satan can do to discourage us, bring it!" Never again will I challenge Satan to "bring it" — because did he ever!

On my third sleepless day of travel, I arrived at the orphanage a day behind everyone else, planning to lead their Sunday church service the next morning and teach at a Bible study for the leadership team of the orphanage the next night. I spent the fourth night propped up on a hard bed, studying and praying — not sleeping — and at 5:30 a.m., I finally began to feel tired. My alarm was set for 6:30 — plenty of time to shower and freshen up before speaking at church — but I slept straight through that alarm and jolted out of bed minutes before we were scheduled to depart. Then, in my haste to get ready, I failed to notice that my cheeks, nose, and forehead were turning red. During that early morning sleep, a spider had marched across my face and bitten me twenty-one times! My cocky challenge, "Bring it!" was starting to actually hurt.

The following day, we traveled to a beautiful bed-and-breakfast that welcomed Christian groups who were doing missionary work. It seemed like the perfect refuge before heading to the remote village of Kamwenge where we would speak at the crusade. But as the fifth night of no sleep was about to descend, fear overtook several team members in a blitz of panic. As we pulled into the guarded beige wall of the bed-and-breakfast after dinner, the sound of wild wolves penetrated the night. The cries of the birds and screeching monkeys, like cries from terrified children, added to the riotous noise. "We can't go on," my team members whispered as we huddled on a bed. "It seems too dangerous. There's too much we don't know."

It is true there was so much we didn't know. As a matter of fact, most of this trip was planned through Facebook messages and a sprinkling of phone calls, hardly a solid itinerary for traveling across the world into dangerous territory. I wouldn't have faulted anyone for retreating; goodness knows the trip was laced with uncertainty, discomfort, and tension. But that night we gained perspective as we prayed and begged God for clarity. We needed hope for the next moment, the next day, the next assignment, for the "Miracle Crusade" in the remote Ugandan village bordering the Congo.

The morning dawned with new promise as we packed our team in a van for a ten-hour drive into obscurity. Back in the United States, Bobby and the other Houston Astros' coaches huddled in their locker room, trying to find our location on Google Earth. As the laptop homed in on our location, they all gasped. "There's nothing around there, Bobby!" they said, shaking their heads in disbelief. "They're in the middle of nowhere."

On our first night in the middle of nowhere, I laid on my bed, deep in prayer and praise, when an urge came over me with a force stronger than a hurricane's. I rushed to the bathroom and spent the entire night hung over the toilet. If I had been at home, I would have been in the ER with an IV drip, that's how sick I was. In the early hours before dawn, panic drove a stake into my heart. "How can I preach today, Lord? I can't even stand up, let alone speak."

Over and over, a phrase from the Bible laid its tonic over my sick body and mind: "power is made perfect in weakness" (2 Corinthians 12:9). Somehow I stood, showered, and went out to speak, not once that day, but three times, to beautiful crowds of people who stood in the African sun over the course of nine hours to hear the Word of God proclaimed. That night as the sun set and the stars came out, I stood on the stage looking over people crouched on a mountain, sitting in the branches of trees, and emerging from the fields of corn in front of us — and all I could do was cry. God had strengthened us. He made our adversaries turn back in shame. I knew I had a couchful of mockers sitting behind me, trembling as they watched the power of God transforming weak American women and stunning African men and women, all of us together longing for a glimpse of his glory.

Every vision has its adversaries, and when they mock, we strike back with the confidence and trust that God is bigger than their taunts. Nehemiah would soon go toe-to-toe with his adversaries, but nothing could thwart his vision. He was at the helm of a watershed moment of rebuilding — and when God brings us to these moments, we're going to start picking up bricks and using them to build.

7

BRICK BY BRICK

Back in the 1960s, my grandparents bought a stunning piece of land hidden deep in the folds of the Rocky Mountains. A small green cabin still sits by a meadow at the base of the mountains, with large peaks rising and falling around it like meringue on a pie. A road pocked with rocks and ruts was the only way to get to the nine hundred acres of sage-kissed beauty.

As we were growing up, my brother, sister, and I looked at every acre as our playground. We explored old farmhouses and abandoned buildings; we walked barefoot down miles of a winding stream; we gasped at the sight of millions of stars speckled across a velvet black sky. It seemed we never grew tired of the magic of that land.

I loved adventure, and one of my favorite things was climbing. I surveyed the mountains around the cabin and determined to climb every one of them within sight. My grandmother loved adventure herself and never seemed too concerned when I'd set off to explore. One day, as I made my way up one of the mountains, I came upon a fence that looked like a little wall deliberately built on the incline.

"Why would someone build something on the steep rise of a mountain clear out here in the wilderness?" I asked my grandma after I made my way down. She explained that the high places of the mountains surrounding the cabin held danger. The wall-like fence had been built decades ago to keep out certain animals and to keep in the cattle they raised. It also helped with the threat of falling rocks and the rush of avalanche snow. What I viewed as interference in my climb was actually a safety net built for our protection.

God has also built walls of protection into the landscape of our lives, walls intended to provide safety, purity, and insulation from the dangers around us. Our walls aren't meant to keep people out — that's isolation — instead they're meant to keep us safe within.

Nehemiah knew the wall he felt compelled to rebuild was more than brick and mortar; it was there for the protection and restoration of a broken people. And if we do an honest survey of our lives and the lives of those around us, we will find plenty of broken walls that need repair.

FROM VISION TO BUILDING

When Nehemiah arrived at Jerusalem, he didn't stand on a rooftop and tell everyone he had come to save the day. He spent a few quiet days surveying the situation. One night he climbed onto a donkey while a few men followed him on foot. They journeyed around the distance of the wall, no small task considering it was the dead of night and the wall was approximately ten miles long.

> Three days after my arrival at Jerusalem I stole out during the night, taking only a few men with me; for I hadn't told a soul about the plans for Jerusalem which God had put into my heart. I was mounted on my donkey and the others were on foot, and we went out through the Valley Gate toward the Jackal's Well and over to the Dung Gate to see the broken walls and burned gates. Then we went to the Fountain Gate and to the King's Pool, but my donkey couldn't get through the rubble. So we circled the city, and I followed the brook, inspecting the wall, and entered again at the Valley Gate.
>
> NEHEMIAH 2:11 – 15 LB

Seeing the extent of the wall's destruction with his own eyes must have been sobering for Nehemiah — sobering, but not deflating, because something happened to him on that night ride. Instead of feeling despair, he seemed to feel excited. Every portion of the torn wall, every pile of rubble he led his donkey around, stirred his faith.

You can always tell someone who has spent time stirring things up with God. They exude a sense that "what is impossible with man is possible with God" (Luke 18:27). Oswald Chambers writes, "God expects His children to be so confident in Him that in any crisis they are the reliable ones."[13]

I've always wanted to be reliable, yet as a teen and young woman, I was anything but. I missed appointments; I let friends down; I was less than trustworthy on jobs — until I fell in love with Jesus. Suddenly, everything seemed to matter. My heart was alert and aware, and being unreliable was no longer an option. When you live for God, your spirit longs to be depended on. It longs to be stirred. But often we sit like cake batter in a bowl — all the ingredients are present, but until we bake them, they simply won't become a cake.

It's from this kind of spiritual stirring that Nehemiah begins to lead. Like a mesmerizing orator, he inspires and mobilizes the Jews to rally around his vision:

> But now I told them, "You know full well the tragedy of our city; it lies in ruins and its gates are burned. Let us rebuild the wall of Jerusalem and rid ourselves of this disgrace!"
>
> Then I told them about the desire God had put into my heart, and of my conversation with the king, and the plan to which he had agreed.
>
> They replied at once, "Good! Let's rebuild the wall!" And so the work began.
>
> NEHEMIAH 2:17 – 18 LB

Spiritual renewal often begins with one person's vision. Nehemiah had a vision, and he shared it with enthusiasm, inspiring Jerusalem's leaders to rebuild the wall. As a study note in the *Life Application Bible* puts it, "Often God uses one person to express the vision and others to turn it into reality."[14]

Earlier I shared how my friend and I had huddled together on a dirty couch, praying through our vision of revival among God's women. It was my utmost desire that God would breathe a fresh breath right over our city, empowering women for his glory and his purpose. What I didn't realize was the effect the vision would have on others. Like a ripple on a pond, the vision started with an initial impact and spread across the calm of the water, leaving it stirred.

Our vision was to host a Monday evening gathering for women, something fresh and authentic, a catalyst to draw women to the real person of Christ. Being a newcomer to the largest church in the country, I knew it was nothing short of a miracle that I was given a platform to teach — and not only a platform but also resources for a band and worship team.

Every Monday morning before dawn, I would drive to the church parking lot and walk across its expanse, praying over every parking spot; I'd then move inside to lie in a crying heap at the base of the stage. I cried in humble adoration of the God who loves vision, begging him to show up, because I knew that if he didn't, I had nothing to say.

The first night, I trembled behind the curtain that was blocking my view of the seats. What if no one came? What if I had the vision mixed up and the timing wasn't right? The doors opened promptly at 6:50, and it was then that I fell to my knees. Women came! They poured in and took their seats; they sang at the top of their lungs; they stayed long after the parking lot lights went off to pray with one another, huddled arm in arm. It didn't take long to see exactly what I hoped for — women experiencing the presence of their Savior, opening their hearts to God's unique vision for each of them. That's the thing about a God-ordained vision — it ignites new vision like sparks from a sparkler, and before you know it, the night sky is lit up with fresh hope.

Watching the Jews rebuild the wall must have been a remarkable sight. Men worked next to women; tribe worked next to tribe; priests and nobles worked next to the lowly — all repairing the part of the wall nearest their homes. People were called to rebuild the portion of wall that most directly affected them, and it would be the portion they would defend when it was finished. It was a brilliant strategy to motivate workers and instill ownership of the task at hand. Everyone had a part in this project—a need and a purpose in rebuilding what was in their own backyards.

The first time I read the book of Nehemiah, I had only been a believer a few short months. I shoved my Bible in a backpack and rode my bike to an elementary school that was abandoned for the summer months. Propped against a wall looking over a playground, I pored over the pages with piqued interest. I sensed this was a book with far deeper meaning than just a story about historical walls. I knew God was speaking to me about personal walls.

I must have read the book of Nehemiah twenty times before I was able to put words to the insight God was revealing. Nehemiah was repairing a wall around a city, and we are repairing the physical and emotional walls around our lives.

WALLS OF PROTECTION

Protective walls are the unseen barriers designed by God to shelter us, a safeguard that steers us toward good choices and sane options. Babies don't have to be told to stop eating when they're full; they just stop. That's a God-given wall of protection. A child who places his or her hands on a hot surface immediately pulls away. They know that burning themselves will hurt—another example of a protective wall given by God.

For some of us, these walls begin to crumble as we get older, the result of others' actions or of our own abuse and neglect. I've spent years examining the causes of the breakdown of my wall. Like Humpty Dumpty, I sat on my wall instead of protecting it, and soon I would have a great fall. Thankfully, "the King" was able to put my pieces together again, but I've learned some costly lessons about broken walls.

When our protective walls crumble by the evil intent of others, it is called abuse. With no say in the matter, some women's walls are in shambles because of pain inflicted on them by another person, circumstance, or cultural trend. Other women's walls crumble by their own dismantling. When our walls start to lose their structural strength because *we* are the ones chipping away at the bricks, three factors are typically involved: compulsion, frailty, and deception.

Compulsion. *Compulsion* replaces normal behavior with abnormal behavior. We almost never jump straight to compulsion — it's a gradual grind. What starts out as an acceptable desire or a pleasurable activity morphs into something forced, strange, or secretive. I saw some of my worst compulsive impulses flare with food. If I enjoyed a particular type of food, instead of sitting down to eat it like a normal person, I would ritually plot how I could binge it. Drive-through windows, pantry escapes, and shoving food in my mouth when no one was looking became my new normal. I moved into the realm of secrets, hiding my behavior so no one else would think I was strange. When I got sick of overeating and what it did to my body, I discovered I was good at dieting. Soon I was struggling with a relentless compulsion that turned smart eating into starving myself.

Where was my protective wall signaling I'd had enough or highlighting the difference between healthy eating and starving? It lay in a heap before me as I walked around it, talked about it, decorated it, and ignored it.

Another of our protective walls has to do with contentment. When this wall is in good shape, we feel satisfied, filled with the sense that what we have is enough. But when we look around at what other people have and feel jealous, our wall is about to crack. People with maxed-out credit cards and piled-up debt are wise to admit that their desire for more has turned to compulsion.

One day I was shopping for a pair of shoes when a woman cozied up next to me and couldn't take her eyes off the shoes I was trying on. Suddenly she blurted out, "I have over a hundred pairs of shoes at home, but I can't stop buying them! Every time I see someone with a cute pair, I feel like I need to buy them for myself." Even though I really liked those shoes, I put them back on the shelf and prayed for the woman the whole way home. (I was tempted to drive back later and buy them, but I resisted!) When our compulsion takes us to this point, the thrill of what we desire lasts for only a short time. Then it's back to figuring out how we can get something new to fill that aching void.

Nowhere do protective walls collapse harder than in cases of substance abuse. Alcohol, painkillers, diet pills, and sleeping pills may all begin as a legitimate help to a problem — but soon the help *becomes* the problem. I can't tell you the number of lovely Christian women who have tearfully shared how that enjoyable glass of wine turned into a compulsive need for more. The need to unwind and ease the tension, to have some "me" time, can turn into a compulsion that bleeds the enjoyment out of anything that was once considered sane.

Frailty. The second reason protective walls crumble is *frailty*. When something is frail, we describe it as weak, feeble, puny, and delicate. I may want my facial features to be delicate, but I definitely don't want my faith to be. It's funny how some of the toughest women I know have the frailest walls of faith. In many areas of life they are uncompromising, but when it comes to their faith, compromise has led to a frail wall that will fall at the slightest push or temptation. These are the women who can't stick to anything. Bible reading, prayer, healthy options, hopeful thinking, and good choices all go south when the first sign of snow appears.

I have a friend who when diagnosed with diabetes was told by her doctor she could reverse the symptoms if she changed the way she ate. Each month for her begins with resolve, but as the weeks tick by, she reverts to her old patterns with food, leaving her sick and frustrated. Lately she has been lamenting, "Oh well, I'll take the insulin since I can't control what I eat." Those of us who love her have reminded her that good health is possible if she can muster up the fortitude to plow through the uncomfortable tension of change. "I just don't have the stamina to stay with it," she sighs — and so she remains sick.

My husband, Bobby, started to chew tobacco at age thirteen. In the world of baseball, this isn't unusual. For some reason it's considered more acceptable than cigarettes because you don't light it and smoke it, but the damage to a player's health and gums is every bit as devastating. Every now and then, Bobby tried to quit but ended up right back where he started, with a chew between his cheeks and gums. It wasn't until his mom died of throat cancer in her fifties that he began to get serious. I looked at him one day and said, "I want to live my life with you for many years to come. I want our kids to have a strong daddy. Can you stop?"

It wasn't immediate, but one day he'd had enough. He asked God to take his desire away and to give him the stamina to stick to his decision. It's been seventeen years since he's chewed, and even though he's around it daily, he has absolutely no desire to touch it. His wall is no longer fragile, and his stamina has remained strong.

The good news is that stamina fights frailty; it wars with procrastination and rationalization. Many of the physical consequences of broken walls (poor health, dull spiritual life, bitter relationships) can be avoided with a vigorous dose of stamina. The stamina to stick to a new behavior, attitude, or choice can be the first brick toward a new wall of strength. Stamina isn't a "grin and bear it" or "just try harder" outlook, but rather the resolve to let God strengthen the parts of our lives we long to see changed. Stamina needs to be rooted in God's work in us rather than in the work we try to conjure up on our own.

Deception. The final reason our walls collapse is *deception*. Though I'm a hater of cons and shams, I've been shoved around by deceit more than I care to admit. Remember the story of the emperor's new clothes? In this tale of deceit, the emperor believes he's wearing a suit made from magical cloth — so magical, in fact, that no one can see it except the wisest of men. Sadly, no one has the courage to tell him he's prancing around in his birthday suit — except for a small child, who blurts out the truth. Suddenly the king realizes how foolish he looks and rushes back to his castle to put on some clothes.

Why didn't anyone tell him he was naked? And why couldn't he see how ridiculous he looked to those observing? Deception thrives when people are afraid to be honest and when we refuse to see ourselves as we really are.

Deceit takes the truth and renovates it. A woman on the brink of an affair may think, "There's nothing wrong with flirting and having a little fun." An alcoholic reasons, "What's wrong with a few cocktails each night?" A beautiful woman stands in front of a mirror and chants, "I'm ugly." Deceit is like cow manure in a pasture; you may not know you're stepping in it until something starts to stink!

Paul warns the Ephesians, "Let no one deceive you with empty words" (Ephesians 5:6), and the apostle John encourages, "Little children, make sure no one deceives you; the one who practices righteousness is righteous, just as He is righteous" (1 John 3:7 NASB). But what about when the one who deceives you is *you*?

One of our toughest battles is overcoming our tendency to deceive ourselves. Self-deception debilitates because it keeps us from seeing ourselves as we really are. When we're wrapped in the blanket of self-deceit, as cozy as it pretends to be, the truth of God is choked out. We entertain lies and rationalizations so readily that we become numb to the freedom of God's whisper. The key to keeping our walls from deceit is knowing the truth so well that when something else is presented to us — a lie, a manipulative compliment, a tempting offer, a rationalization — we aren't intrigued. The truth is far more interesting.

Last spring I was preparing to teach a group of women a lesson on rebuilding walls. For days, Bobby and I collected large cardboard boxes to build a wall in front of the stage where I was speaking. The wall was a sight to see — about three feet high and thirty feet wide, and we covered it in paper to look like stone. Then I placed sticky notes on every chair in the room. At the end of the lesson, I invited women to write on their sticky notes what they longed to rebuild in their lives, to notice where deceit had taken hold, and to dream of a new wall being created. It was stunning to see a thousand women placing sticky notes on this wall and bowing in prayer — some quietly weeping and others heaving sobs so loud that you could almost hear heaven crying.

We didn't touch the cardboard box wall that night — it was too holy to tear down immediately. We collected the anonymous sticky notes in a folder the next day, and nothing prepared me for the depth of the pain reflected in these notes.

- *I need you to rebuild my wall of self-worth, God. I need your love, not all the material things I've convinced myself I need, and now I've driven myself into debt.*
- *I'm feeling lost and unsure of the direction of my life due to infertility. Please rebuild my wall of purpose.*
- *Sexual abuse has broken my wall. My only worth has been giving sexual pleasure to men. Please, God, heal and rebuild my brokenness.*
- *I want to be free from the love and misuse of food. I pray for a new wall of freedom to be built around my behaviors so I'll view food like my children, who respond to their inner signal and would never think of overeating. I want to be FREE!*
- *God, I need a wall of faith, confidence, and lack of fear as I move forward without my beloved husband. For fifty years he held me up, guided me, and protected me with love. How can I live without him?*
- *I have no direction. I'm ugly, useless, selfish, and unimportant. I won't ever be fulfilled. Can you rebuild this wall of self-hate?*

As I look again at these sticky notes, tears stream onto my laptop. I wish I could huddle with each of these women and infuse them with hope as we cry over the broken state of their walls. Although I can huddle, only Jesus can heal.

In the gospel of Luke, a few short sentences describe the way in which Jesus often rebuilds walls. The religious people were watching him closely. You know the type — they criticize with their eyes when you try to confess; they separate themselves when things get too complicated; they imply that asking for healing is too dramatic, as if to say, *Is your life really that bad?*

A man suffering from abnormal swelling in his body sat before Jesus, and Luke reports, "Taking hold of the man, he [Jesus] healed him and sent him on his way" (Luke 14:4). That's the simplicity of how Jesus works. He takes hold of us. He literally grabs us from our mess and hugs us, and then he heals us. Sometimes the healing is immediate — a fresh perspective, a restored body, a change of circumstance. Sometimes it comes gradually — a mended heart, transformed habits, altered attitudes. This rebuilding, however, always points to the same end — being sent on our way. We're not shoved away; we're led away by Jesus himself, newly equipped with maturity and an understanding of the redemption he is thrilled to give us. Like the Jews in Nehemiah's day, we're scared and unaware of the simplicity of God's restoration. But without it, all things remain crumbled. With it, however, all things are possible.

LITTLE FOXES

As the new wall around Jerusalem began to take shape, the two politicians who had made fun of Nehemiah and the Jews were outraged. Sanballat screamed out to his associates and the army of Samaria, "What are those feeble Jews doing? Will they restore their wall? Will they offer sacrifices? Will they finish in a day? Can they bring the stones back to life from those heaps of rubble — burned as they are?" (Nehemiah 4:2). Sanballat's buddy Tobiah joined the bashing as he joked, "What are they building — even a fox climbing up on it would break down their walls of stone!" (Nehemiah 4:3).

It's interesting that Tobiah uses a fox to describe how stupid he thinks their building project is. The fox is usually described in cartoons and fables as sly, tricky, and conniving — a perfect depiction of the way Satan tries to destroy the walls we want to rebuild. How many of us have tried to rebuild a negative attitude we have about a situation only to end up thinking worse thoughts than when we started? That's a fox at work! Have you ever tried to undo a habit you know brings destruction and yet find yourself more deeply entangled in it? That's a fox!

Do you hear yourself rehearsing the same lines over and over like an iPod stuck on play? "You'll never be different." "This is the best you can hope for." "You're too messed up and phony to be used by God." That's a fox! These cunning creatures make it their priority to prance on our walls with fear and doubt, leaving us inactive, paralyzed, defeated. Wily and cruel, their main goal is to derail our watershed moment, to convince us we never had one in the first place.

Sanballat and Tobiah didn't stop there. They were so angry the Jews were following through with the rebuilding that they began to plot how they could stir up trouble by fighting against them. But Nehemiah wasn't going to let his workers languish in failure. He shooed the foxes off the wall and faced the challenges with bold intentionality.

Nehemiah acknowledged the damage. He faced reality. He didn't pretend the comments made weren't hurtful or frightening. "But we prayed to our God and posted a guard day and night to meet this threat" (Nehemiah 4:9).

Nehemiah focused on the work, not the threats. "So we rebuilt the wall till all of it reached half its height, for the people worked with all their heart" (Nehemiah 4:6).

Nehemiah submitted a strategy to protect the people from attack. Strong leaders implement the things others only talk about.

Therefore I stationed some of the people behind the lowest points of the wall at the exposed places, posting them by families, with their swords, spears, and bows. After I looked things over, I stood up and said to the nobles, the officials and the rest of the people, "Don't be afraid of them. Remember the Lord, who is great and awesome, and fight for your families, your sons and your daughters, your wives and your homes."

When our enemies heard that we were aware of their plot and that God had frustrated it, we all returned to the wall, each to our own work.

NEHEMIAH 4:13 – 15

Fifty-two days later, Jerusalem's wall was rebuilt. What had lain in an embarrassing heap of rubble for years was rebuilt in fifty-two days! For those of us who love the hope of positive change happening fast, there's nothing more delightful than this picture.

When the seventh month came and everyone was settled in their towns, over forty-two thousand people assembled in front of the Water Gate to hear the scribe Ezra read from the Book of the Law of Moses. As he opened the book, the multitude stood to their feet, but before he could even begin reading, they began to shout, "Amen, Amen!" while lifting their hands. The next thing they knew they were bowed low, worshiping the Lord with their faces to the ground. Tears streaming down dirt-stained faces, these Jews were welcoming their watershed moment. As their chests heaved, sobbing from the significance of this moment, they had to fall to the ground.

Seeing God move on your behalf has a way of doing this. When you feel the magnitude of God's goodness, standing is no longer an option. I can't tell you the number of times I've ended up with my face on my kitchen floor, my bathroom tile, or the steering wheel of my car. These are moments when our faces can't handle the weight of his glory.

Nehemiah and Ezra encouraged the people to stop weeping, to get up and eat and drink, for this was a day holy to the Lord. Nehemiah shouted to the people, "Do not grieve, for the joy of the LORD is your strength" (Nehemiah 8:10).

After the hard work of rebuilding walls, it's time to celebrate, and no one enjoys celebrating more than God. Imagine the joy in churches if people gathered for the sole purpose of celebrating the moments of God's victory in our communities of faith. Food, laughter, music, praise — engaging one another and enjoying our God. If we labor with him to rebuild what is broken, the joy of the Lord will be our strength. It's a strength that can't be contained or measured, for it floods our lives with the torrents of his grace.

Part Four

THE
WATERSHED OF
CONTROL

8

TRYING TO BE KING

The other day, I sat at a stop sign for ten minutes watching a mama duck leisurely cross the road with her ducklings. Traffic piled up a mile behind me as this mama kept her brood in check. Not one duck wandered from the line as her watchful eye seemed to keep them on an invisible leash. Each duck was in step, marching forward and following mama as each webbed foot waddled in perfect formation. "Wow," I thought with a giggle. "This mama has it together. She literally keeps her ducks in a row!"

With cars honking behind me and my patience fraying inside of me, I rolled past this family feeling a bit jealous. I've tried so hard to keep *my* ducks in a row, only to see them scatter in a tattered mess of squawking confusion. My bent toward control and an insatiable need to fix things has left me in the middle of traffic on more than one occasion.

One night I stood on stage and illustrated this to the women in my Bible study. I had placed some cute rubber ducks in a perfect row on a wooden bench. I explained that to God, our little rows of ducks usually end up anywhere but in perfect formation. One by one, I swatted them from the bench — but I had no idea how far they would travel! One little ducky shot into the air and knocked over one of the letters that spelled out the title of our study — *WATERSHED*. The *S* went tumbling down and left us with a disheveled *WATER-HED*. Every fiber in me wanted to walk over and fix that sign, but I didn't. I let it stand there the entire night — mixed-up and broken. I had more than one e-mail the next day from control-loving women like me, lamenting how hard it was to not get up and fix it! That's why I love women; we understand our need to be mama ducks and keep the people and details of our lives in a row. To God's amusement, our lives never seem to line up.

In his book *The Purpose Driven Life*, Pastor Rick Warren rephrases C. S. Lewis's words from *The Great Divorce*: "There are two kinds of people: those who say to God '*Thy will be done*' and those to whom God says, '*All right then, have it your way.*'"[15] How I long to be the first kind of person, because I know that God's way is always better than my way. Since the first woman, Eve, walked the earth, our struggle has been wanting to be in charge.

When God spoke to Eve after she chose the forbidden fruit, he said something that has stuck in my craw for decades. He told Eve, "Your desire will be for your husband, and he will rule over you" (Genesis 3:16). The word *rule* makes my blood chill. I don't like to be ruled. I don't even like plastic rulers! They remind me of straight lines that can't be free or creative. Why in the world would a husband be awarded the task of ruling me? What if I don't want to be ruled?

After fervently studying the word *rule* and trying to make sense of God's intent, I've realized I have a poor mental image of the word because I've only seen it play out negatively. I associate the word with men who are mean, pushy, or manipulative — those who lord it over women rather than treasuring them. John and Stasi Eldredge describe what happens when this type of "rule" is out of whack:

> When a man goes bad, as every man has in some way gone bad after the Fall, what is most deeply marred is his strength. He either becomes a passive, weak man — strength surrendered — or he becomes a violent, driven man — strength unglued. When a woman falls from grace, what is most deeply marred is her tender vulnerability, beauty that invites to life. She becomes a

dominating, controlling woman — or a desolate, needy, mousy woman. Or some odd combination of both, depending on her circumstances.[16]

When I think about the men who shaped my view of manhood, their résumés are less than impressive. After my dad's car accident, he went silent. I hardly ever heard him speak. He was dealing with a load of pain so massive that you could feel the heaviness just by glancing at him. He had lost the use of his legs; he had lost his position as bank president; he had lost the respect of his wife — and for many years, he had lost the will to live. Wrapped in that coat of pain was a family that still needed him, but his silence kept us out. After trying to snuggle in that coat with him but feeling rejected, I did what most young girls eventually do when they can't make sense of their parents' pain; I quit trying. Regrettably, I began to form an opinion of men that stuck with me even after my husband and I were married. I believed that men were expendable. Women didn't really need them because typically they will hurt you, leave you, restrain you, or shut down in front of you.

When I married Bobby, I thought I could dictate what part of my heart I would allow him to know, and what part I'd keep for myself. Somehow I thought I could categorize our love like a clothing catalog: this section is for people to see (we're dressed up and looking good), this section is intimate apparel for only the two of us to see, and this section is where he does his thing and I do mine — no need to put a male model on pages that belong to women. Shoo!

I'll never forget when after a year or two of marriage Bobby sadly confessed, "You don't need me." Somehow in my sophisticated defense mechanism, I believed the lie that I could marry a man and not really get involved. My need for control suffocated my need to be vulnerable.

Women who are vulnerable are neither weak nor pushovers; they are the perfect balance of a heart willing to trust and a spirit willing to hope. When we are hardened and dominant in our love for a man, we've forfeited our femininity in order to "feel safe and in control," as

John and Stasi Eldredge remind us.[17] Sadly, "safe and in control" usually translates to "lonely and manipulative." I've seen many women play on the playground of control, only to wake up one day miserable and alone. It's a playground we want to run from, and if we've been a fixture on its swings and slides, we need to leave, no matter how high we've swung or how fast we've slid.

Interestingly, the same word, *rule*, is used to describe our submission to Christ. "Let the peace of Christ rule in your hearts, since as members of one body you were called to peace" (Colossians 3:15). The true fragrance of this word isn't the stench of power but rather servant-like protection — the type of protection that brings peace.

Within the safety of this kind of rule, we were designed for significance — but this leads to a fundamental question that haunts and prods women, one that's been passed down through the ages and pushed from one generation to the next: Are we vulnerable enough to let go of being a controller so that we may become an influencer?

We are meant to influence, to have a godly impact for good on those around us. Control wears the mask of influence, but it kidnaps influence and ties it up. After some punching and kicking, it leaves influence with tape over its mouth, hands, and feet. Unable to speak and prevented from moving, influence is crushed in the wake of control — yet influence is the potent purpose of a woman's life. The greatest influence God has designed for a man's life after God's own relationship with the man is a woman. Notice that in the garden, God didn't create a bunch of buddies, a board of directors, or a posse for the man to consult after his season of being alone; he created a woman, meant to be his greatest source of influence and his staunchest ally. Why in the world have we become adversaries?

A WOMAN NAMED JEZEBEL

In Scripture, no one struggled with control issues quite like Jezebel did. She proudly ruled over her husband, her household, and a kingdom with unbridled cockiness. Her name possibly means "the prince [Baal] exists," and she did everything in her power to force the worship of this false god on everyone. Whenever God's people wandered in their worship, they wandered toward Baal (Numbers 22; Judges 2 – 6), whose pagan worship involved sacrifice — often human. Worship of Baal also led to sexual immorality, as female and male attendants performed sexual acts to bring fertility on themselves and the land. Jezebel was raised in a culture that loved this pagan god, and she brought her upbringing with her when she married Ahab, the king of Israel.

With the force of a tsunami, she crashed through the landscape of the kingdom, leaving men quivering in her wake. One of the men she left shaking was the prophet Elijah. A man's man if there ever was one, he ran for the hills when she threatened him after he killed the false prophets in a fiery showdown proving that the Lord was God (1 Kings 18 – 19). Her power and dominance knew no boundaries, especially when it came to her twisted relationship with her husband.

Ahab wasn't a sissy. He led armies and fought wars — but the Bible describes him as a man who slumped into a wimpy whine when things didn't go his way. When he couldn't acquire a vineyard that bordered the palace property, he plunged into a moody mess.

> Some time later there was an incident involving a vineyard belonging to Naboth the Jezreelite. The vineyard was in Jezreel, close to the palace of Ahab King of Samaria. Ahab said to Naboth, "Let me have your vineyard to use for a vegetable garden, since it is close to my palace. In exchange I will give you a better vineyard or, if you prefer, I will pay you whatever it is worth."
>
> But Naboth replied, "The LORD forbid that I should give you the inheritance of my ancestors."
>
> So Ahab went home, sullen and angry because Naboth the Jezreelite had said, "I will not give you the inheritance of my ancestors." He lay on his bed sulking and refused to eat.
>
> 1 KINGS 21:1 – 4

There he was, king of a nation, sulking on his bed because of a vegetable garden! But there's more to the story than vineyards and veggies.

Naboth was a God-fearing Jew, and the land he owned had been passed down for generations, as the law commanded (Leviticus 25:23; Numbers 36:6). Ahab had no interest in this kind of respect for God and took it personally when Naboth refused to bargain. When Jezebel walked into their bedroom and saw him sulking on the bed, she was perplexed and disgusted.

> His wife Jezebel came in and asked him, "Why are you so sullen? Why won't you eat?"
>
> He answered her, "Because I said to Naboth the Jezreelite, 'Sell me your vineyard; or if you prefer, I will give you another vineyard in its place.' But he said, 'I will not give you my vineyard.'"
>
> Jezebel his wife said, "Is this how you act as king over Israel? Get up and eat! Cheer up. *I'll* get you the vineyard of Naboth the Jezreelite."
>
> 1 KINGS 21:5 – 7, italics mine

The essence of control has its root in the word *I*. Notice Jezebel doesn't take this moment to remind her husband that he is king or that he doesn't really need that vineyard. Notice she doesn't encourage him or speak words to lift him up. She emasculates him by saying, "This is the way a king acts?" and then shows her real colors by barking out, "*I'll t*ake care of it!" (in other words, "I'll do it because you're incapable and no one can do it as well as I can"). Instead of influencing him for good, she controls him for chaos.

OVERCOMING THE "I" SYNDROME

Before I beat Jezebel upside the head with my Bible, I'm reminded of the times I've done the very same thing. The "I" syndrome is fueled by the solitude of the word *I*. "I" doesn't play nice with friends. It likes to be in charge and in control. I'm embarrassed to recall the times my husband has offered, "How can I help?" My reply, all too often, is, "I don't need help." "I'm fine. I've got it covered." "I'll take care of it." "I" rarely lets other people in because "I" thinks it will do a better job than others will do; or it's afraid that other people might not be sincere in their offer to help. The funny thing is, the more I function in the "I" syndrome, the more I feel like a martyr. *I'm so tired. I'm so frustrated. I feel so alone.*

Several years ago, I was so overwhelmed in the world of "I" that I had to step back and reevaluate the way I lived. Bobby was managing teams in the minor leagues, far from our home in Colorado. His job took him away an average of eight months a year, so I was quite efficient at solo parenting. I entered the teaching force when our youngest child went to preschool, and a decade later, I was deeply immersed in my career, kids' sports and activities, ministry opportunities, and household responsibilities. I would push myself until I had nothing left at the end of each day. When the kids had a problem, I proudly took charge of it; when there was an issue at work, I volunteered to help find a solution; when something went wrong at the house, I fixed it; when people struggled spiritually, I vowed to help them change.

All this sounds noble, but at times I found myself wondering if I was doing the right thing. I seemed to jump in too quickly to rescue my kids — talking to teachers, smoothing out schedules, making sure they weren't uncomfortable. At work I was breaking my back to keep up, working a nine-hour day after church on Sundays to be ready for the next week. Spiritually I had all the right answers to cheer people on to freedom and victory, but I felt exhausted and overwhelmed when they didn't seem to change quickly enough for my "Amen!"

One day I woke with the same ache in my muscles that was becoming an unwelcome companion and made an appointment to see my doctor, hoping to get a quick fix so I could continue to strap the world on my shoulders. My blood work came back skewed, so he sent me to a specialist, hoping we could figure out what was going on. I was diagnosed with two autoimmune diseases that were squeezing me from the inside out, and it took this squeezing to shake the "I" syndrome right out of me. No longer could I function with the "I can do" mentality. As a matter of fact, "I can do" turned to "I can't without help!" This was a watershed revelation. The world will still rotate even if I don't try to spin it. It was during this time that I let God truly take over — to be the heartbeat and purpose behind all I did. Frankly, I didn't have the energy for anything but his grace.

During this time of surrender, I noticed a few interesting things take place: my kids became more adept at handling issues in their lives; at work, new people stepped up to the challenges we faced as a staff; and spiritually I learned that my role is to *lead* people to the living water, not to *be* the living water for everyone who's in need. I was breaking free from the "I" syndrome that had choked my trust in God for far too long.

Sadly, women like Jezebel never break free. Typically, they end up only making worse the situations they try to fix. And true to the pattern, Jezebel was about to turn a whining desire from her husband into a monumental tragedy.

DAMAGE CONTROL

When Jezebel told Ahab, "Don't worry about it. I'll get you Naboth's vineyard!" she meant business. Quickly, she wrote letters in Ahab's name and sent them to the civic leaders in Jezreel, where Naboth lived. She told them to ask the people to come together for fasting and prayer, wickedly making her request sound spiritual. Once the people gathered, she told the leaders to single out two bad men and have them falsely accuse Naboth of cursing God and the king. The punishment for this was death, so after Naboth was falsely accused, he was dragged outside the city and violently stoned to death.

When Jezebel heard the news, she proudly said to Ahab, "You know the vineyard Naboth wouldn't sell you? Well, you can have it now! He's dead!" (1 Kings 21:15 LB). Instead of being repulsed by her actions or saddened that his immaturity had led to the death of an innocent man, Ahab did the most cowardly thing imaginable — he was silent. No comment; no remorse. Sometimes silence is the loudest response we give.

He got what he wanted, and after letting his wife run wild with control issues, *he* didn't have to harbor the blame for an innocent man's death. After all, it wasn't *his* name signed on the decrees; it was *hers*. If we're honest, women struggle with control in ways much like men struggle with passivity. There may be some areas in which a man is totally alive — work, friendships, sports; at the same time, there may be other areas where he lies passive — the kids, household duties, his wife. This sets up a cycle that rinses itself out regularly in the form of fights and frustration. A woman controls when a man is passive, and the more he's passive, the more women control. Then, after both man and woman have left a trail of tears, we settle into blame.

I never realized how damaging blame is until my marriage fell apart. Bobby was my prince, and after ten good years of marriage, I thought we were bulletproof, protected from the pain and secrets that tarnish many professional athletes' lives. He was chapel leader of almost every team we played on, and I was the Bible study leader, quite firmly convinced that if someone prayed hard enough and believed boldly enough, they'd be sheltered from the things they were scared of.

The one thing that scared me to death was infidelity. I had watched countless women break down in the wake of discovering the man they had committed their lives to was unfaithful. I saw the devastation of adultery in my mom's life and verbally vowed to hit the road if this torment were to ever touch me. I threatened Bobby in a sweet way. "You know, babe, if that ever happens, I'll be gone faster than you can blink, so be good ... OK?"

The night he told me he had been unfaithful, I felt like Chicken Little realizing that the sky actually *had* fallen. Who was this man whom I deeply loved but obviously didn't know? I beat myself up for my ignorance and chided myself for letting my guard down with men.

"See, I told you men were dangerous," Satan whispered to me. "You never should have given yourself away to him."

Bobby assured me that a woman can only know what a man allows her to know, and he had destroyed the gift we'd spent ten years of marriage building: trust — trust in God, trust in love, and trust in the power of the two becoming one. Now my trust lay before me like burned toast, and no amount of butter and jam could mask the awful taste I was left with. I saw no alternative but to throw my burned toast in the trash.

The problem was that I loved him. It wasn't a needy, victim-type love but rather a love that envisioned him as the man I hoped he would one day be. As we sat slumped on a counselor's couch in the foothills of the Rockies, we uncovered a truth that changed the trajectory of our lives. We had a watershed moment that bloomed like an epiphany: He blamed me.

I was in utter disbelief. "You blame me for *what*? All I've done is pack up and follow you around this country, helping you fulfill your dreams in baseball. What about my dreams?" I cried. "What have I done to deserve your blame?"

When you're dealing with a pain that deep, nothing seems to make sense — and this mixed-up mind-set was a whopper. His blame toward me could be traced back to a single decision to buy our first house in New Jersey, the state most Yankees called home during the baseball season. After the birth of our first child, we decided to buy a home and forsake a bit of our nomadic lifestyle. I fell in love with a house I saw in the first week of looking, and a few months (and some womanly persuasion) later we bought it. He acted happy and excited, but deep inside he harbored the belief that we should move to a warm climate in the off-season — a place sort of like his childhood home in southern California, a place where he could work on his baseball skills year-round. Instead of voicing his concern, he was passive, tucking away the option to blame me if his career didn't pan out as we hoped. Bobby didn't sit around concocting sinister blame plots; this was a subtle, sneaky excuse that pushed itself forward when he was most susceptible.

The crazy thing is that I would have gladly bought a home somewhere warm to preserve his career. I loved the home we bought in New Jersey — it used to be a chicken farm, and the home had hardwood floors and a sunroom — but nothing meant more to me than his security as a ballplayer. But placing my security in Bobby's ball playing was part of the problem too. I needed to look squarely in the mirror and ask myself, "Do I love Bobby the man or Bobby the ballplayer?" Somehow over the years everything seemed to get muddled. Nothing *ever* warrants a man straying from his wife and their vows, but in the wake of this pain, I knew I had to own my part of the mess if we ever hoped to heal from it.

As Bobby recognized his decision to blame and the devastating fallout from adultery, I came to a realization as well that I loved the man, not the ballplayer. We prayerfully allowed God to stitch our hearts back together and promised to never again let blame or passivity call the shots in our marriage.

Blame calls the shots in a variety of ways that may at first glance seem harmless, but if nursed and encouraged, blame does nothing but divide.

You're the reason I didn't fulfill my dreams.
You've got me trapped in family responsibilities and obligations.
It's your fault I look the way I do.
I'd be happy if you didn't make so many stupid decisions.
You don't meet my needs.

If we're not careful, we may find ourselves blaming others for everything from job failures to low self-esteem. Eventually, blame finds a way to shoot its arrows at God. Adam struggled with this in the garden after he chose to join his wife in sin. When confronted with his choices, instead of taking responsibility for his passivity in not protecting her, he blamed God. "The woman *you* put here with me — she gave me some fruit from the tree, and I ate it" (Genesis 3:12, italics mine). So now it's God's fault, because if he hadn't given Adam the gift of a woman, none of this would have happened! That's the logic of blame — never look at yourself and your own behaviors; just keep pointing fingers at someone else.

King Ahab pointed the finger of blame too. Somehow he felt entitled to any piece of land he wanted, and he blamed the godly man Naboth for defying his request. He passively watched his wife murder an innocent man and later blamed Elijah for confronting him with the truth of his actions (1 Kings 21:20). When it comes to blame, there are no boundaries. It roams wherever it pleases, spouting excuses and finding fault.

Sometimes I wonder what might have happened if Ahab and Jezebel had gone to counseling. What if they allowed a watershed moment to change them from being passive, immature, and controlling to being loving, honest, and gracious? What if Jezebel had welcomed her role as influencer rather than controller? The course of their family history may have been radically different. Sadly, Jezebel's daughter acted in the very same way she'd seen her mama act — out-of-control controlling.

In the next chapter, we'll spend time with a biblical role model who got it right. She loved God and had great political power, but she never lost sight of her purpose — to influence those around her to fervently trust God.

9

INFLUENCE,
NOT CONTROL

Influence is often misunderstood and undervalued. Described as the ability to inspire, impact, sway, or guide — why do we prefer to stomp, speak out, organize, or rearrange? Influencing someone may be the most powerful thing we ever do, but there are a few things we should note about its power, though you won't see them noted in headlines or articles. You may not see immediate results from godly influence, and it's possible you won't ever receive thanks, even though your guidance has been profound.

I recently read a story that describes the power of such influence.

Rufus Jones often told a story from his childhood: It seems that one day when he was 12 or 13, his mother went to town, leaving him behind on the farm with some chores. He fully intended to do the work, but his friends' beckoning to play grew too loud.

When he saw his mother's car pull into the driveway that evening, his heart sank. He knew he was in for one of the worst whippings of his life. His mother parked the car and came into the house. She looked him straight in the eye. She didn't have to ask.

Rufus said he would always remember what happened next. It affected him as no whipping ever could. His mother took him upstairs into the bedroom, knelt down beside him, wrapped him in her arms, and, with tears streaming down her face, prayed one phrase over and over: "Lord, make a man out of him. Lord, make a man out of him."

It is said that whenever Jones told that story his voice would grow quiet, his eyes misty, as he remembered that special feeling of "standing in the weeping arms of love."[18]

Rufus's mom chose influence over anger that day, and her boy was impacted by it for the rest of his life. Although her actions were intentional and concise, I doubt that as her knees hit the hard floor beside her son's bed she could have foreseen the power her influence would have. Women of influence don't care about power; they just want to encourage outcomes.

Susanna Wesley is said to have spent one hour each day praying for her seventeen children. What's more, she took each child aside for a full hour every week to discuss spiritual matters. It isn't surprising, then, that two of her sons, Charles and John, were used by God to bring blessing to all of England and much of America.[19]

Sometimes when I read about inspiring women, I feel like a failure. Would I have yelled at my son for not doing his chores? Would I bustle through my days trying to cook, clean, and survive in a household of seventeen children rather than praying for their fruitfulness? As I mulled this over in my mind, a quote from Dan Allender and Tremper Longman came to mind: "Our greatest privilege is shaping the character of the soul to reflect the image of Christ ...We are called to disciple one another; that is, we are called to participate with God in shaping one another to reflect more gloriously the beauty of God."[20]

Suddenly it all makes sense. To influence is to shape, to offer words, advice, prayers, and love for a grander purpose — to bring forth the beauty of God in someone else. We're appointed as mothers, wives, girlfriends, daughters, coworkers, teachers, neighbors, and classmates to be influencers who help shape the image of God in others.

After my first book, *Truly Fed*, was published, I began regularly teaching classes on the topic of disordered eating. Michelle was a woman who nestled into a seat in the back. She kept her eyes low and rarely made eye contact with me. I assumed she didn't like the material, but I felt compelled to walk toward her when the class was over and give her a hug. The embrace was awkward, but with her eyes still fixed on the floor, she whispered, "Maybe there's hope for me after all."

She explained that it had been a hard road that led her there. Anorexia and the shame of undereating, then overeating, kept her wrapped in frustration. But food was a mere Band-Aid on a bigger, oozing wound. After a painful divorce from a violent man, she endured stints in a mental hospital where she underwent shock therapy to try to jolt her depressed mind into a state of well-being. I took her trembling hands and told her I was sure that God had more than hope for her; he had purpose.

We met after classes to pray and often met for coffee, where we'd talk about her life, her fears, and her hopes for the future. In time, I asked her to run a book table, serve on my advisory board, and share her struggles and triumphs with other women. Eventually Michelle became a coleader of "Truly Fed" classes, using my book and DVD series to facilitate classes long after I moved out of state.

When I think back to the friendship I had with Michelle, its hallmark was influence. I was given the gift of influencing her life, helping her to see beauty and purpose as a beloved woman of Christ. It was never my intent to keep her in her place, with she being a student and me being a teacher, she as the one needing healing and me as the one doling it out. Often that's how we feel — like a project someone is working on rather than a woman being loved.

A woman of influence builds with her words. She places no personal agenda on the glory that God brings in people's lives, because his agenda exceeds any counsel or encouragement she could ever give.

A WISE INFLUENCER

One of the Bible characters I greatly admire is a woman named Deborah. A true influencer, she never missed an opportunity to inspire rather than control.

Deborah was both a judge and prophet, which is truly remarkable when you consider that in her day a woman's role was to take care of her family and little else. Judges were the ruling governors in Israel, shouldering the spiritual, political, judicial, and military leadership of the nation, while a prophet was someone God chose to communicate his will to the people. Besides Deborah, only Samuel is mentioned as both prophet and judge, which confirms that her titles were a big deal.

In addition to serving as a judge and prophet, she was married to a man named Lappidoth, who was also a judge. Although both members of this powerful couple held important roles in Israel, Deborah is the one whom Scripture focuses on as a woman of influence.

Rabbis who came on the scene centuries later were disturbed by the Old Testament's portrayal of Deborah. These men tended to have a negative view of women and were bothered by the fact that her role elevated her above men's status. The name Deborah means "honey bee," but these rabbis tried to render her as a "hornet," implying that she was a woman who overstepped her boundaries. But this wasn't true. There's no misunderstanding the people's love for her and the way God used her to lead a nation.[21]

The first time she's mentioned, we see her sitting under a palm tree in a place designated as her personal courthouse. This was where she listened to people's disputes and made judgments about their problems.

> Israel's leader at that time, the one who was responsible for bringing the people back to God, was Deborah, a prophetess, the wife of Lappidoth. She held court at a place now called "Deborah's Palm Tree," between Ramah and Bethel, in the hill country of Ephraim; and the Israelites came to her to decide their disputes.
>
> JUDGES 4:4 – 5 LB

The shade of her palm tree provided more than judgments; it provided the setting for wise counsel regarding the military strategy of the nation. It was to this place that she summoned Barak, the head of the army of Israel, and shared with him what the Lord had shown her.

> "The LORD, the God of Israel, commands you: 'Go, take with you ten thousand men of Naphtali and Zebulun and lead them up to Mount Tabor. I will lead Sisera, the commander of Jabin's army, with his chariots and his troops to the Kishon River and give them into your hands.'"
>
> Barak said to her, "If you go with me, I will go; but if you don't go with me, I won't go."
>
> "Certainly I will go with you," said Deborah.
>
> JUDGES 4:6 – 9

I love the flow of this conversation. When Deborah shared her vision of a military strike, Barak could have responded in a variety of ways — after all, he was a commander. He could have asked questions; he could have argued; he could have been silent and filled with fear. Instead, he says something so expressive that you can almost feel Deborah's influence swaying in the palm trees. He simply says, "If you don't go, I won't go. That's how much I trust God's strength within you."

One of the things I admire about Deborah is that she knew her boundaries of skill and influence, and she stayed within them. She was not a military leader, and she never pretended to be. After receiving a strategy from God describing the course of the battle, she called on the one who was meant to lead it — Barak. If she had been a controller, she might have tried to lead the military charge herself. Instead, she appointed someone who already was a leader and built him up. This leads us to a trait we want to stop and notice: *Influencers know how to build other people's potential rather than thinking they have to take on every challenge themselves.*

I have to sit with this one for a while. Being a supercharged "doer" who moves through the day at the speed of light, I've forced myself to reflect on the times I could have influenced but chose not to. One of the reasons I believe women don't build potential in others is they're afraid those others may surpass or replace them.

I once worked with a staff of teachers as a consultant for the Public Education Business Coalition. After trying a few new approaches in a classroom I'd been guest-teaching in, the teacher pulled me aside and whispered, "Don't share these ideas with the rest of the staff because then my class won't stand out as excelling." My jaw nearly hit the floor when I realized she wanted to keep this exciting strategy to herself so *she* could excel rather than her staff and students. Instead of being a force of influence among her peers, she wanted to hoard praise and recognition.

Sadly, I see this in ministry too. As I shared earlier, for twenty years I yearned to write books, but every time I mentioned my desire to published authors or established speakers, they flew into a litany of despair, reminding me that the odds of publishing a book are about as good as a Little League team winning the World Series. I'd shake my head in frustration, until one day my faith in God exceeded my faith in opinions. I forged a path that was gutsy and tenacious in my quest to get published, and God honored my belief that it could be done, regardless of how hard it would be to get there.

To this day, whenever I hear someone so much as mention a desire to write, I pour out everything I know in order to help them. I meet with them, encourage them, and pray for them. I give them any tool I know about to help them on the path.

I once heard an author say, "We're all just feeding the lake. Jesus is the water, and every writer, speaker, pastor, Bible study leader, worship leader, publisher — we're just feeding the lake." No lake feeder is more important than another, and there's room for everyone to succeed. The result is a lake that nourishes and refreshes multitudes, not puddles and trickles of individual effort. If you're busy trying to maximize other people's potential, God will maximize yours.

BACKSTAGE INFLUENCE

Another thing I love about Deborah is how she positioned herself when it came to battle. She knew Israel needed to see Barak as the military leader, so instead of sitting on a chariot in front of everyone, she slid into the background, praying and believing for victory. She knew her role and didn't try to flaunt her importance. Barak himself said, "I can't do this without you!" Wisely she rested in the role she was meant to play. This leads us to the second trait we want to note: *Influencers are comfortable both in front of people and in the background because they realize* they *aren't the point* — God *is.*

After Deborah shared her initial vision with Barak, she added something: " 'Certainly I will go with you,' she said, 'but because of the course you are taking, the honor will not be yours, for the LORD will deliver Sisera into the hands of a woman' " (Judges 4:9).

At first glance, it looks like she's had a prideful moment — scolding Barak by telling him he won't get the victory but instead a woman will. But she wasn't being prideful, nor was she singing a chorus of "I am woman, hear me roar!" She was sharing a deeper prophecy, one that revealed a third party who would bring this victory home — an insignificant woman named Jael.

It was Jael who hid fleeing Sisera under a rug in her tent and later hammered a peg through his head while he slept (Judges 4:21). She was an unlikely warrior, but in the end, her influence over circumstances brought Deborah's prophecy to life.

Not one of the leading actors in this drama was more important than the other. And God rightfully got the praise because *his will* was the point, not furthering his followers' spiritual résumés. Influencers love nothing more than seeing God receive a standing ovation.

Throughout history, no one knew how to influence like Jesus. It was never his style to push to the front of the line to get noticed. Instead, he influenced his followers to serve. After an emotional string of days in which he received the news of his cousin John's death, healed throngs of sick people, and turned measly rations into a meal for thousands, instead of climbing into a boat to rest while his disciples sent the people away, he put *them* in a boat and personally dispersed the crowd (Matthew 14:22). I've often wondered if the disciples didn't learn more from that act than they did from a year's worth of teaching.

Or how about the image of Jesus cooking fish on the beach after his resurrection (John 21:9)? He knew his disciples were aimless and looking for comfort, so he prepared a picnic to meet their needs. You'd think they would have prepared a meal for him, but instead he stooped by a fire to cook fish himself. He is called the Son of God and the Son of Man, but I like to call him the Son of Influence. He understood that an act of humility or a word of truth can sway the hope of mankind. Maybe that's why his name is the name whispered when people hurt, when they're lost, or when they're about to take their last breath. His influence is still the most compelling prize on earth.

A WATERSHED SONG

Deborah's love for God is just as prevalent after the Israelites' victory as it was before they stepped onto the battlefield. In a moment revealing the exquisite humility of influence, Deborah and Barak experience a watershed. With voices pronouncing the triumph of God, the first thing they do after victory is sing.

> So may all your enemies perish, LORD!
>> But may all who love you be like the sun
>> when it rises in its strength.

JUDGES 5:31

Notice the essence of their song isn't about the battle or even about the victory. Instead, it's a hymn that sheds promise over the life of every person who loves God — that we may be like the sun when it rises in its strength. The breath of this song brings us to the final trait of those who influence: *Influencers allow God's strength and purpose to be the most important descriptor of their lives.*

I tend to roll my eyes when people say things like, "What would you want someone to write on your tombstone?" Tombstones are for the dead, but we are among the living. Maybe the question should be, "What would people write on a sticky note if they were asked to describe you? Right here, right now — what would they say?"

I remember a time when I got to read this type of sticky note, and it came in the most unlikely way. On a Tuesday night in August, I was leaving the room where we'd just had our wives' Bible study. A precious group of wives and girlfriends had been meeting for months in a lower-level room at the Astros' stadium in Houston while our men slugged out games above. That night was particularly sweet as we circled our conversation back to the love of God. I reminded the women that to grow they needed to be intentional, pushing away from stagnant faith to a fearless trust in God. Our group was always running from fear — fear of failure, fear of rejection, fear of unfaithfulness, fear of being replaced. We stood hand in hand, weeping as we prayed, holding each other before the throne of grace. It was a night marked by delicate tears, reminding us that God took on human flesh, and he dwells among us.

As we finished praying, I hugged the wives and walked alone through the tunnel to the family room where the children of players and coaches are watched by child care staff. I'd brought our granddaughter to the ballpark to give my pregnant daughter a night off, and as I entered the room, a familiar face stood in front of me. I called her Miss Virginia, a beautiful caramel-colored woman who ran that nursery like an admiral runs a ship. It was clean, efficient, and ready for the next game in tip-top shape. I gave her a quick hug and thanked her, as I always did, for providing a haven for the kids so we could have our Bible study. She graciously smiled as I scooped up my granddaughter and prepared to leave.

That night, before Bobby and I even pulled into our driveway, we got a call from the team's general manager letting us know we were fired. When you've been in the game for over thirty years, you know that endings come with the territory, so we ended the call and thanked God for the years he had given us with the Astros.

Leaving a job abruptly doesn't allow for proper good-byes and, sadly, I never went back to that stadium I had spent many years in. But one day I received a message that brought me to my knees. It was a message from Miss Virginia:

Good morning, Ms. Gari,

Words cannot express how I felt when I found out what happened. The ladies and I were really sad when we heard the news. You have been a true ray of sunshine to the family room and the organization. We are going to miss your smile and kind words and your way of letting us know we're doing a good job. We're going to miss your family.

I personally want to thank you because there were days that I just wanted to walk away from it all, but you would come in and then that thought would disappear. Your spirit is so engaging, and I thank you for sharing it with us. Thank you for what you have done for the family room staff and for what you have done for me.

God bless,
Virginia

I bawled when I read this note — not because of the beauty of her words or because I was proud of anything I had done. I cried because all I had done was notice. It was so simple to tell her thank you and to appreciate who she was. I didn't even realize that influence was seeping through. Although I didn't know Virginia well, our time together was painted with purpose.

I reread her note, trembling and on my knees, because in the pain of getting fired from a team I loved, I was having a watershed moment — a moment in which I felt the full impact of the influence of a word, a smile, a hug, an affirmation.

The joy of influence flows from the spirit of who you are; you don't sit around trying to stir it up. We don't save this for special events or tombstones, because there are too many people who need an influencer in their lives now: a child who needs direction, a friend who needs some truth, a spouse who needs to feel valued, a leader who needs a mentor. Influence has the ability to breathe new life into limp sails. It enables those it touches to glide toward new horizons.

Part Five

THE
WATERSHED OF
APPROVAL

10

THE PRESSURE
TO PLEASE

People who say, "I don't care what anyone thinks!" are lying to themselves. All of us are, to some degree, pleasers. It's part of our nature to please because it's part of the nature of God. Consider the third day of creation — just one day in a span of six — and notice the word that best describes God.

> Then God said, "Let the water beneath the sky be gathered into oceans so that the dry land will emerge." And so it was. Then God named the dry land "earth," and the water "seas." *And God was pleased.* And he said, "Let the earth burst forth with every sort of grass and seed-bearing plant, and fruit trees with seeds inside the fruit, so that these seeds will produce the kinds of plants and fruits they came from." *And so it was, and God was pleased.* This all occurred on the third day.
>
> GENESIS 1:9 – 13 LB, italics mine

God was pleased. He wasn't proud, tired, or expectant; he was pleased — the same type of pleased he felt when Jesus emerged from the waters of the Jordan to the joyful bellow, "This is My beloved Son, in whom I am well-pleased" (Matthew 3:17 NASB). If God is a pleaser, shouldn't we be too?

Pleasing God and others should be genuine and spontaneous, but as a recovering people pleaser, I know my desire to please has not always been pure. It seems the notion of pleasing often gets confused with compromise, and in an effort to be pleasing, we mistakenly give away its pleasure.

Many women bulldoze their way through life — being reckless with words and actions, ignoring how they affect those they encounter on their path. These women are covering sores, having tried to please parents, husbands, friends, or bosses, and ending up maimed instead. Being mean becomes a comfortable retreat from the painful effort to please.

The flip side to a mean retreat is a desperate commitment to satisfy others. I've learned the hard way that there will always be someone you can't please, and believe me, I've tried! Pastor and author Rick Warren writes these words:

> Many people are driven by the need for approval. They allow the expectations of parents or spouses or children or teachers or friends to control their lives. Many adults are still trying to earn the approval of unpleasable parents. Others are driven by peer pressure, always worried by what others might think. Unfortunately, those who follow the crowd usually get lost in it.
>
> I don't know all the keys to success, but one key to failure is to try to please everyone. Being controlled by the opinions of others is a guaranteed way to miss God's purposes for your life.[22]

I feel no shame in saying I've been a people pleaser most of my life. To be pleasing to people is one of life's great joys, but we get in trouble when pleasing people supersedes pleasing God.

When I was five, I wasn't the most attractive girl in kindergarten, mostly because I struggled with allergies, and my nostrils were often a bright shade of green. Because I was a bit shy and unsure of myself, friends and playmates weren't plentiful — until a strange twist of fate seemed to bring good fortune my way.

My dad was a young banker, and often his work took him to banks out of state while my mom took care of me and my two-year-old sister. Late one night, as Mom and I were asleep in my bed, we heard a crash that sounded like an airplane screeching off a runway. Our small house backed up to a major highway, and instinctively Mom knew something was terribly wrong. We slipped on our robes and tiptoed out of my bedroom to find a mangled car in our kitchen! A drunk driver had lost control as his car careened off the highway and into our home. If that car had swerved twelve inches to the left, it would have slammed into the nursery where my baby sister slept.

The next few days were a blur of excitement. It isn't often that a neighborhood experiences a car in a kitchen, so naturally the kids on the surrounding blocks wanted to take a peek. Suddenly, everyone liked me!

I formed small groups and led scheduled tours through the house for days. No matter what time someone knocked, I wanted to show them around because it seemed to please them. It wasn't until my dad pulled me aside and said, "Honey, no more tours," that I felt my world fall apart. Now the kids were mad at me because I couldn't deliver. When they knocked, I had to let them down, and letting someone down feels like death to a person who wants to please.

And so at the tender age of five, I took an internal vow to do whatever I could to gain people's approval. Three decades later, I renounced that vow, worn-out and bruised by trying to make everyone happy and feeling as though I'd compromised the very essence of the word *please*.

In Good Company

The apostle Peter had a problem with people pleasing; maybe that's why I love him like no other. It seems there are traits in people who are prone to please that other personality types don't contend with. Think about the differences between Peter and the apostle Paul. They approached life from two very different perspectives. One perspective isn't better than another, just different — and God uses different temperaments to illuminate his purposes. Do you see yourself in either of these temperaments?

COMPARING PAUL AND PETER

Paul	Peter
Sensible	Compassionate
Thorough	Thoughtful
Logical	Whimsical
Practical	Idealist
Problem Solver	Visionary
Speed Walker	Group Hugger

You can probably guess whom I identify with. Thankfully, I married a Paul. My husband is Paul to a tee, and he scrunches his face in disbelief when I lament about failing to please someone or letting someone down. He simply asks, "Gar, did you do your best?" I typically nod yes with a sad look pasted to my face. "Then that's pleasing to God," he assures me.

I know why I'm bent internally toward pleasing, but I often wonder why Peter was. Why would a brawny fisherman from Capernaum fall prey to the empty echo of approval? A look at two time frames in his life sheds light on this question. The first is an *ego boost timeline* filled with events that could inflate an ego faster than helium filling a balloon; the second is a *pleaser timeline* that signals it's time for the balloon to pop.

INFLATED EGO

In the course of three chapters in the gospel of Matthew, Peter experiences a watershed moment, finally grasping the remarkable idea that he is traveling with a Savior and beginning to sense that no power on earth can compare to what his fisherman eyes and ears are now privy to.

If we were to lay the events from Matthew 14 – 16 on a timeline, it would look something like this:

EGO BOOST TIMELINE

| 5,000 fed | Walking on water | 4,000 fed | "Rock and church" praise from Jesus |

It started with a day of intense healing. Tucked in a desolate place away from villages and the buzz of commerce, Peter stands in stunned silence after Jesus tells the multitudes he's been ministering to (somewhere around ten to fifteen thousand people, including women and children) to sit down. He then takes five small loaves of bread and two fish, and somehow multiplies them to feed thousands.

> As evening approached, the disciples came to him and said, "This is a remote place, and it's already getting late. Send the crowds away, so they can go to the villages and buy themselves some food" ...
>
> "Bring them here to me," [Jesus] said ... Taking the five loaves and the two fish and looking up to heaven, he gave thanks and broke the loaves. Then he gave them to the disciples, and the disciples gave them to the people. They all ate and were satisfied, and the disciples picked up twelve basketfuls of broken pieces that were left over.
>
> MATTHEW 14:15, 18 – 20

I can just picture Peter walking through that crowd giving high fives. There's nothing like making people happy, and hungry multitudes experiencing a miracle will surely bring smiles all around. It's energizing to be on a winning team, and at that moment, "Team Jesus" was number one to everyone involved. Picking up those leftovers must have felt like winning the lottery. Slaps on the back, "Way to go!" ringing in his ears, Peter was in a good mood when he got on the boat that was to take the disciples to the other side of the lake.

Later that night, Peter would get another ego boost. After being tossed and tumbled in a storm for nearly nine hours, Peter and the disciples see something coming toward them on the water. "It's a ghost!"

they shout. But once they realize it is Jesus, Peter courageously asks
him to call him out onto the water.

Sometimes I wonder if Jesus was grinning with a fatherly pride
when he yelled back, "Come" (Matthew 14:29). Peter wasn't testing
God when he asked to climb out into the stormy sea; he was flexing
his faith — something that always makes Jesus proud. So with flexed
faith and a drenched robe, Peter walks on waves.

Because we're familiar with this story, we may lose the magnitude of
its wonder. A human being walking on water! The craziness of this statement lodges somewhere between impossible and nuts, in my mind. And
although Peter began to sink, panicking, after he lost sight of Jesus, Jesus
grabbed him, and the wind died down as they climbed into the boat.

Can you imagine trying to sleep that night while replaying the feel
of a wave's crest beneath your feet? Somewhere in the secret recesses
of his mind he had to be thinking, *I did something no one except Jesus
has ever done!*

My hunch is that he woke up the next morning reasoning, "I
walked the waves with Jesus, and my friends are amazed by my courage." He's basking in the warmth of the disciples' approval, and the
small ego of a fisherman isn't so small anymore.

And then soon after walking on water, Peter enjoyed being part of
a mountainside crusade.

> Jesus left there and went along the Sea of Galilee. Then he went
> up on a mountainside and sat down. Great crowds came to him,
> bringing the lame, the blind, the crippled, the mute and many
> others, and laid them at his feet; and he healed them. The people
> were amazed when they saw the mute speaking, the crippled
> made well, the lame walking and the blind seeing. And they
> praised the God of Israel.
>
> MATTHEW 15:29 – 31

There's nothing better than being around people who are amazed.
This crowd was so giddy about what they were experiencing that they

began praising the God of Israel, and Peter was right in the middle of their praise. He wasn't the one being praised, of course, but he was a part of the addictive excitement that spreads like the tide taking over a sandy beach.

And now Jesus is about to make the three-day retreat even better. With seven loaves of bread and a few small fish, he calls down the power of heaven to amaze this crowd once more.

> He told the crowd to sit down on the ground. Then he took the seven loaves and the fish, and when he had given thanks, he broke them and gave them to the disciples, and they in turn to the people. They all ate and were satisfied.
>
> MATTHEW 15:35 – 37

Now that they all had healed bodies and full stomachs, I imagine Peter couldn't shake the feeling that his Savior was off the charts in popularity and goodwill. He knew he was a part of a winning campaign, the golden grail of acceptance to one who loves praise. Peter had seen Jesus move in the masses *and* within his small band of disciples, but something was about to blow these events away. He was about to have a face-to-face encounter with Jesus that would revolutionize his self-image.

When they arrived in Caesarea Philippi, Jesus asked his disciples who people thought he was. The answers varied, and then Peter's words cut through like a laser: "You are the Messiah, the Son of the living God" (Matthew 16:16). This answer pleased Jesus.

> Jesus replied, "Blessed are you, Simon son of Jonah, for this was not revealed to you by flesh and blood, but by my Father in heaven. And I tell you that you are Peter, and on this rock I will build my church, and the gates of Hades will not overcome it. I will give you the keys of the kingdom of heaven; whatever you bind on earth will be bound in heaven, and whatever you loose on earth will be loosed in heaven."
>
> MATTHEW 16:17 – 19

Talk about an ego boost. Jesus blows Peter's socks off. He's given Peter the keys to the kingdom, for heaven's sake. It doesn't get much better than that! Jesus' words to Peter are laced with praise, confidence, and a plan — the same way he speaks to us if we have the fortitude to listen.

I've learned that those God chooses to lift up are only elevated so *his* name can receive praise, not so they can feel better about themselves. When I was younger, my lines between ministry and self-help were easily blurred. Oswald Chambers writes these words:

> The test of our spiritual life is the power to descend; if we have power to rise only, something is wrong. It is a great thing to be on the mount with God, but a person only gets there in order that afterwards they may get down among the devil-possessed and lift them up ... The mount is not meant to *teach* us anything, it is meant to *make* us something.[23]

There's nothing glamorous about mucking around with people covered in spiritual mud. But if you want to be useful, you need to get dirty. It's not all glory and keys to the kingdom, as Peter would later understand. It's more about sacrifice, humility, building up others instead of yourself, working tirelessly with excellence, and letting Jesus take center stage while so many things are at work to upstage him. I'm embarrassed to admit that pushing myself to the forefront always ends in disappointment.

I remember a time I decided to push myself center stage before God chose to place me there. I took it upon myself to contact the head of a women's conference for professional athletes, and I explained to her that I was the right person to teach a workshop, listing my qualifications with blatant assurance. The woman in charge of the conference was faithful and godly, a true model of leadership, and after some tender questions about the extent of my healing on the topic she wanted taught, she agreed to let me teach.

The day I was to speak I couldn't move out of the fetal position. I tried to go to the scheduled events of the morning, but I was in so much emotional pain I couldn't leave my hotel room. Sitting in a hot bath forty-five minutes before I was to speak, I knew I was trying to wash my pain away. I stood before a room filled with Major League wives, and I bawled through every point I was trying to make. I never saw an evaluation from the workshop, but I would guess that I left every woman there in a state of panic. I was in no shape to teach on a topic I hadn't even settled into myself. I had no hope to offer and no wisdom to share — just a trash can full of Kleenex from a gushing fountain of grief I couldn't seem to turn off.

I learned something invaluable at that conference as that watershed moment of reckoning exposed my need for approval. The Lord showed me parts of myself I'd been hiding from — that I'd rather teach about something than feel it, that I'd rather look like an authority than a student, and that I'd rather be out in front than down at the feet of Jesus.

Another layer of my approval-seeking heart had been exposed, and although it took me years to get over the embarrassment to my ego, God has given me a new heart that longs for his purpose rather than for praise.

Popular Peter was about to fall off his mountain of accolades into a valley of authenticity, and another type of timeline would take the place of the one that had simply built his ego — a timeline that skillfully replaced approval and applause with humility and worship.

11

LOVE PEOPLE — BUT PLEASE GOD

The events of the last chapter left Peter's ego boosted. Who wouldn't enjoy helping to feed thousands, walking on water, and being called a "rock" by Jesus? Peter loved the status, the attention of the crowds, and the feeling that everyone was pleased with him and the agenda of the One he followed — Jesus. This is what I call *people-pleaser's bliss*, a type of ecstasy in which people are happy with you, your family, and your endeavors. The trouble is that it never lasts. A misunderstood comment, an oversight, or a family member's less-than-friendly action can turn your bliss into a blizzard!

Peter was about to enter a snowstorm so intense that it nearly buried him in an avalanche of self-doubt. That's the problem with people pleasing; once the favor and pats on the back have stopped, it's hard to define who you are without them. Through a series of events on a *pleaser timeline*, we'll see Peter's bent toward approval fall apart as Jesus exposes him. Like grapes that must be crushed to produce a fine wine, Peter's life would be squeezed and changed.

MUDDLED POPULARITY

Immediately after Peter's "rock" conversation with Jesus, circumstances seem to take a nasty turn. Over the course of five events, Peter's penchant toward pleasing is wrecked.

PLEASER TIMELINE

Rebuke by Jesus	Disciples' ranking	Transfigura- tion spotlight stealing	Denials	Tiff with Paul

Peter was still flying high from the conversation that set him apart as a leader, but when Jesus began talking about the persecution and murder he would soon face, Peter panicked.

> From that time on Jesus began to explain to his disciples that he must go to Jerusalem and suffer many things at the hands of the elders, the chief priests and the teachers of the law, and that he must be killed and on the third day be raised to life.
> Peter took him aside and began to rebuke him. "Never, Lord!" he said. "This shall never happen to you!"
> Jesus turned and said to Peter, "Get behind me, Satan! You are a stumbling block to me; you do not have in mind the concerns of God, but merely human concerns."
>
> MATTHEW 16:21 – 23

The very thought of Peter taking Jesus aside to rebuke him makes me shudder. Although many commentaries spin this as Peter caring so much about Jesus that he didn't want him to suffer, another undertone whispers through his concern. Peter is really saying, "I don't want you to suffer because then *I* have to suffer. Popularity is great. Why mess this up?" The vibe around Jesus is changing. It's about to get messy and unfavorable, and for a people pleaser this feels like torture.

Jesus goes straight to the source of Peter's undertone by addressing Satan himself. We could swirl in many directions around this one, but for the sake of addressing Peter's pleasing nature, Jesus named Satan as the author of misdirected approval seeking. He even went so far as to say, "You set your sight on human approval, not God's."

Imagine how Peter the rock felt when Jesus looked right past him and spoke to Satan! What about the keys to the kingdom? What about the foundation of the church? In one brief sentence, Jesus starts to unravel Peter's internal fabric — a fabric tightly woven with the threads of people pleasing.

THE FOUR THREADS OF PEOPLE PLEASING

As I see it, four threads characterize this need for approval and pleasing:

- **Thread #1:** Pleasers want things to be smooth, free from turmoil or conflict — no matter the cost.
- **Thread #2:** Pleasers often sacrifice purpose for performance.
- **Thread #3:** Pleasers need approval in order to cover a scar or a lonely heart.
- **Thread #4:** Pleasers often find themselves in a compromising state because they're trying to accommodate several viewpoints.

Thread #1: Don't Make Waves

Making waves is the worst thing a person prone to pleasing can do. Because we hate conflict, the presence of waves means someone isn't happy, and we'll do whatever it takes to keep smiles on people's faces. Most of the people I know who struggle with this grew up in homes where there was some kind of turmoil or undercurrent of harsh expectation. Children learn to dance a strange and delicate dance when peace is at stake, and I became a world-class dancer.

When we were young, my sister and I would do the grocery shopping for our family. We would ride our bikes to the store a few miles away, and after paying for the groceries, we filled our large backpacks with food and then hung the paper bags around each of the handles of our bikes. This allowed for about eight bags of groceries to be transported in one trip.

One day it began to rain, and all of a sudden our bags were waterlogged as we littered the road with our food — a cereal box here, a chunk of cheese there. We quickly jumped off our bikes and began gathering our groceries as light rain turned into a downpour. We knew we couldn't afford to leave the groceries on the side of the road (food stamps helped pay for them), so we did the smartest thing we could think of — we hid them under someone's bushes. Sheepishly we climbed back on our bikes and made our way home.

As we pulled onto our street, I had a familiar sick feeling in the pit of my stomach. Would Mom be mad we didn't make it home with the groceries? What if the home we left them at belonged to someone who would be angry because we trespassed on their property? I was so tongue-tied that I could barely get the words out as we explained what happened.

Mom had just entered Alcoholics Anonymous a few weeks earlier, and as we climbed into our car to hunt down our food, I thanked God she didn't seem mad — just slightly annoyed. We led her to the yard where our groceries were stashed, and as we pulled up, Mom let out a gasp. The house with the bushes was the home of her newly appointed AA sponsor! Like secret agents, we crawled under the bushes, grabbed the groceries, and lunged for the car.

As we pulled away, I watched my mom's face, desperate to see how she would respond. For years I had based my behavior on her moods and comments, and I learned that in a family already beaten down by heartache, I'd do anything to keep things smooth. Slowly a smile began to form on my mom's face, and before we pulled into our driveway we were all giggling as we plucked leaves and twigs from our food items.

I'm thankful for my mom's sober reaction that day because I know I would have crumbled — *I'm so sorry! We should have held the bags tighter! It's my fault!* — if she hadn't shown us grace. When you're an approval junkie, you want to sidestep conflict, no matter the cost. And usually the cost is your self-worth.

Thread #2: Purpose or Performance?

Six days after Peter's rebuke, he was in for another blow. Jesus invited James, John, and Peter to climb a mountain with him. Huddled together on that mountaintop, these three men were about to witness something

so supernatural that human eyes and minds could barely take it in and
make sense of it. As they crouched between rocks and sage, Jesus began
to glow. Revered prophets, dead for centuries, were talking to Jesus as if
they were visiting with each other at a church function.

> After six days Jesus took with him Peter, James and John the
> brother of James, and led them up a high mountain by them-
> selves. There he was transfigured before them. His face shone like
> the sun, and his clothes became as white as the light. Just then
> there appeared before them Moses and Elijah, talking with Jesus.
>
> MATTHEW 17:1 – 3

The disciples were witnessing a moment so holy that to speak
would spill the passion right out of it. But never one to miss a moment
to speak, Peter begins spilling.

> Peter said to Jesus, "Lord, it is good for *us* to be here. If you wish,
> I will put up three shelters — one for you, one for Moses and one
> for Elijah."
>
> MATTHEW 17:4, italics mine

James and John are speechless, drenched in the vision of a glowing
Savior and prophets they've loved from their youth. But Peter blurts
out, "Lord, it's good for *us* to be here." Suddenly Jesus is no longer the
point; *they* are.

Quickly, Peter shares what he can do to make that moment even
better. "I'll build tents!" It's in that moment that God the Father puts
the focus back on Jesus, as his voice booms out through the clouds surrounding the mountaintop: "This is my Son, whom I love; with him I
am well pleased. Listen to him!" (Matthew 17:5).

God had to speak a holy *shhhh* to Peter. Be quiet! This moment
isn't for you to build something for me; it's so you can *be* something for
me. Pleasers tend to confuse this, and thus they often sacrifice purpose
for performance.

Nothing that happened on that mountaintop was scripted; it was

Jesus' moment to shine, to be filled and ministered to by Moses and Elijah. When Peter offers to make tents, he wants to stand out by "doing" something for God. Although some commentators feel this moment reflects Peter's desire to serve Jesus and the heavenly visitors, it seems to me that serving in this moment shifts the focus from Jesus to a performance-related task. But performing for God is futile because he doesn't want our performance; he wants our hearts. We don't have to work to please him; he's already pleased.

I can honestly say I've wrestled with this concept more than any other in my life. I have worked myself into a frenzy trying to please God, only to hear him say, "My grace is sufficient for you, for my power is made perfect in weakness" (2 Corinthians 12:9). What freedom it is to know that *his grace* is what makes me strong, not working harder or desperately trying to please!

When my son entered sixth grade, I had a watershed moment. Sitting at my kitchen table, I uncovered a pattern of "performance pleasing" I had laid on his small back since he was young. Colton had the "gift" of having his mom teach at the elementary school he attended, and I'm sure some days it felt like a curse. He couldn't sneeze without me knowing about it.

Shortly into his second-grade year, he was recommended for the gifted/talented program. I was certain he was both gifted and talented, and although we wouldn't have the test scores to prove it until the next year, I was thrilled to have him included in this elite group.

Colton lived for recess more than anything else, and there were three things that meant the world to him as he grew up: football, basketball, and baseball ... period. At first he liked being part of the G/T program, but as the years progressed, the work got harder, and he didn't want the stress of more work alongside his sports commitments. Although he was getting all As and an occasional B, I insisted he stay in the program. Looking back, I realize that I wanted to keep his G/T teacher happy with me. She was strong and smart, and I enjoyed our professional relationship so much that I didn't want her to be mad at me or my son. So year after year, he'd beg for relief, and I made him stay in the program.

I hit an all-time low when Colton was assigned a major writing project in fifth grade, and I did what all good parents do when their child balks at something: I bribed him. Instead of allowing him to grow, struggle, or look bad in front of his teacher, I helped him *significantly* on this project. Let's put it this way: I was a professional writer at the time, and although I didn't write his entire project for him, he heavily consulted me on how to write it!

By the time Colton entered sixth grade, I was exhausted. At the beginning of his first year in middle school, the G/T teacher at his new school contacted us about grafting him into their program. Colton slumped in his chair. "Not again, Mom!" he moaned. This time I prayerfully knew my people pleasing had to stop. I calmly said, "No problem. You make whatever choice you think is best."

That day I jumped out of the competitive grades race, the race where parents are pushing and kids are sweating. I moved away from the G/T label to the "average grades" label. For some reason, Colton's grades fell after that day. Instead of As, he made Cs and Bs, with a D here or there in high school — but I knew *he* owned those grades, not me.

So Bobby and I practically fell over when in college Colton was on the dean's list for academic excellence three straight years! When I asked Colton what made the difference, he replied, "I finally figured out all the things you used to tell me about teachers and students, and I loved knowing these grades were mine, not yours." It felt good to quit pushing my son for a stellar performance — and even better to quit performing myself.

Thread #3: Approval That Covers Scars

The next stop on the pleaser timeline doesn't single out Peter specifically, but we can infer that he's in the midst of the action. As the disciples travel with Jesus, they approach him one day and ask, "Who, then, is the greatest in the kingdom of heaven?" (Matthew 18:1). In other words, they were looking around at each other like students vying for positions on student council. "Who's going to be student body president?" "Who's vice president?" "Which losers won't get a title at all?"

In the kingdom of humanity, accolades and positions of honor signal strength, but in the kingdom of God, humility is strength. Jesus quickly calls over a little child to make his point.

> He called a little child to him, and placed the child among them. And he said: "Truly I tell you, unless you change and become like little children, you will never enter the kingdom of heaven. Therefore, whoever takes the lowly position of this child is the greatest in the kingdom of heaven. And whoever welcomes one such child in my name welcomes me."
>
> MATTHEW 18:2 – 5

I can picture the look on the disciples' faces as Jesus stroked the hair of the child in his arms, their eyes searching the ground for relief from their self-centered need for approval. As a study note in the *Life Application Bible* puts it, "We are not to be *childish* (like the disciples, arguing over petty issues), but rather *childlike*, with humble and sincere hearts."[24] Children are naturally trusting. They are weak and dependent on their caretakers, and they're meant to be. You don't see three-year-olds venturing out on their own, pushing other kids down so they can rise to the top and stand out. They just want to be loved by their parents, and this is what Jesus says kingdom approval should look like.

The disciples thought a ranking in heaven would make them feel better about themselves, and sometimes we look for labels to cover the scars of a lonely or unappreciated life. Think of the labels we attach to our lives — mommy, Mrs., executive, leader, teacher, president, captain. I've worn all these labels, and never have I felt complete in them.

In my book *Spirit Hunger*, I call these scars on our lives "spiritual scar tissue." Wounds that have left us hurt, banged up, or bleeding have a way of surfacing when we think about a difficult childhood, a painful work experience, a devastating event, or a relationship that's left us

broken. It's through a bloodied wound that people pleasing often fes-
ters, and the wound can be hard to clean out. Wound-infected pleasing
can look like:

- fear of letting someone down
- fear of not being excellent or the best
- fear of trying, because you're sure you can't win approval

My friend Jenna shared a story I pondered for weeks. She struggled
with fear while living with a wound so deep that no amount of people
pleasing could heal it. With honest reflection, Jenna opened her heart:

"The saying 'not all things are as they seem' may sound trite, but
this was a phrase that turned out to describe what I *thought* was going
to be a perfect life. I was raised in a loving Christian home and saw life
through different shades of rose-colored glasses. I was an optimist, and
I saw my future as a beautiful canvas, ready for life to stroke with its
colorful brush. When I married after college, I settled into a life that
my friends and family envied — but after seven years of marriage, I
discovered that 'not all things are as they seem.'

"My husband had a secret — a secret that virtually ripped me to
shreds. The shredding wasn't immediate, but rather like a slow rip
that pulls and tugs. The more he tore, the more I tried to be perfect to
please him. Instinctively I knew something was wrong with our relationship. We were friends, parents, and companions — but we weren't
lovers — and I internalized this rejection as I tried harder to please.
He finally admitted he'd struggled with homosexuality throughout our
entire marriage. Years of his perfectionism and my inability to please
him became clear.

"What made matters worse was because he wasn't 'out' with his
sexuality, he asked me to keep his secret from his family, our children,
and our friends. While my family and a few personal friends knew the
truth, I floundered in the midst of unwarranted criticism and scrutiny
for my failed marriage. His family turned their backs on me, blaming me
for breaking the perfect marital record his family liked to boast about.

"In the midst of this dark time, God began to minister to my deepest needs. He caressed my throbbing questions, 'Will I ever be loved?' 'Will I ever be enough?'

"It was in the throes of this pain that I had a watershed moment. I've always loved the comfort of the Scripture in Jeremiah 29:11: 'For I know the plans I have for you,' declares the LORD, 'plans to prosper you and not to harm you, plans to give you hope and a future.'

"But it was the words following this verse that spoke to the depths of my spirit: 'You will seek me and find me when you seek me with all your heart. I will be found by you,' declares the LORD, 'and will bring you back from captivity' (Jeremiah 29:13 – 14).

"I was in captivity to a person — trying to please and never feeling like enough. God began to show me that *he* was enough, and over the course of time I witnessed a healing so profound that only a watershed could have invited the change. I was able to forgive my ex-husband, and to this day we have a real friendship. But the biggest gift came in the man I went on to marry and now call husband. He's my soul mate and the one who treasures my beauty as a woman. Each day I look at him, I'm reminded there isn't a valley dark enough or low enough that's beyond God's reach for rescue. I don't have to toil to be pleasing; my life is pleasing to God, and the man I share my life with is pleased too."

Jenna's story reminds me of a lunch date I witnessed between a daddy and his four-year-old daughter. When they sat down at the table next to me, I could see the eyes of this child dancing as she looked at her daddy. Between bites of food she would stand and render a ballet move for her daddy to watch. "Look, Daddy," she'd coo, as she twirled and lifted her leg in an arabesque.

Daddy would smile and say, "Great, sweetie! How about some more mac and cheese?" She'd take a bite and then stand to show him another move. After she seemed to tire of showing off her dance moves, she looked at her daddy and said, "Daddy, I think I want to sit on your lap." He scooped her up and cuddled her as they ate. Although this daddy enjoyed watching his daughter try to please him, what I think he loved most was holding her on his lap. I wonder if we need to crawl onto our daddy's lap and enjoy eating the mac and cheese he's given us.

Thread #4: Whom Do We Please?

There's no doubt the low point of Peter's life took place in a courtyard outside the building to which Jesus was taken after his arrest. In one tense evening, he denied knowing the Lord he had pledged his life to (Matthew 26:69 – 75). What would cause a man to deny knowing someone he loved? How could he swear allegiance to Jesus, and hours later swear he doesn't know him?

Peter's collision with people pleasing left him nowhere to hide. That cold night, he ransomed his love by pretending ignorance. "I don't know him" rang bitterly in his ears as he ran from the courtyard, looking for a place to collapse and weep. In the anxious moments by the fire, Peter chose to present himself unattached and unaffiliated. What's worse is his pleasing nature succumbed to the approving eye of servant girls and bystanders — people he didn't even know.

Sometimes I try to imagine what Peter's days looked like after these denials. Did he shut himself up in a room, replaying the denials that so easily flowed from his fickle heart? Thankfully, it's never Jesus' intent to allow our lives to get stuck on replay. Peter was noticeably absent until after the crucifixion, but Jesus made sure to restore Peter's confidence when they had breakfast on the beach before Jesus' ascension (John 21:15 – 17).

The all-time low of denying Jesus was Peter's catalyst toward change, a change that strangled his people-pleasing pride and rebuilt a God-pleasing faith.

THE LURE OF COMPROMISE

The last stop on our pleaser timeline leads to a prickly place of compromise. After Jesus ascended, Peter was carrying out his role as church leader. No one could work a crowd like Peter, and it seemed as though he was perfectly suited for the ministry God had given him. Peter was a tower of strength for the first Christians of the early church — but just when we think we're beyond something we struggled with in the past, it can reappear and remind us to be keenly aware of our misguided tendencies. And Peter's tendency toward people pleasing resurfaced with a vengeance.

After Jesus' death, one of the principles God had to make clear to the Jews was an inclusive policy. Up until then, the Jews were the particular recipients of God's favor, and although they were loved by God, he wanted *all* people to know his favor — which included the Gentiles. For a Jew like Peter, this wasn't easy to swallow, but after experiencing a vision in which the Lord showed him that all foods were clean — crushing the thought that Jews could be favored by what they ate (Acts 10) — Peter changed his approach and freely invited Jews and Gentiles to the family of God. But somewhere between grace and tradition, Peter fell back into his old ways.

When Peter spent time with James (a very Jewish disciple and traditional thinker) and a band of Jewish Christians who held to circumcision as a symbol of right standing with God, he seemed to float down the stream of their beliefs, actually separating himself from Gentiles who weren't circumcised. It wasn't until the apostle Paul confronted him about it that Peter was jolted back to an awareness of his need to please.

> When Cephas [Peter] came to Antioch, I opposed him to his face, because he stood condemned. For before certain men came from James, he used to eat with the Gentiles. But when they arrived, he began to draw back and separate himself from the Gentiles because he was afraid of those who belonged to the circumcision group. The other Jews joined him in his hypocrisy, so that by their hypocrisy even Barnabas was led astray.
>
> GALATIANS 2:11 – 13

Peter ran smack into a cultural clash and couldn't figure out which side of the fence he stood on. I once heard a speaker say, "If you don't stand for something, you stand for nothing," and right then Peter was in the middle of nowhere, standing for nothing. His heart knew the truth, but his actions proved he was afraid to follow it, so he stood between two fences, desperate for approval from certain believers. Pleasers often find themselves in a compromising state because they're trying to appease several viewpoints. Have you ever tried to please two types of people?

- wild friends and your church family
- a demanding mother and your sweet husband
- struggling children and a mean teacher
- a full calendar and your exhausted family

It's easy to flip-flop in mushy compromise when you're trying to please too many people. The good news is that Peter accepted Paul's reprimand and changed. He had his watershed moment, and from that time on, we don't see any more waffling. As a matter of fact, in one of his later writings, Peter shares with Christians who have been dispersed and persecuted, "Therefore humble yourselves under the mighty hand of God, that He may exalt you at the proper time, casting all your anxiety on Him, because He cares for you" (1 Peter 5:6–7 NASB).

I wonder if the anxiety Peter mentions has to do with trying to please. For all his quirks and shortcomings, Peter was arguably Jesus' best friend on earth. I adore Peter because I'm so much like him. If Peter were asked to share his life motto as his days on earth drew to an end, I think he would have said, "Love people — but please God."

Part Six

THE
WATERSHED OF
OVERCOMING

12

WHEN GOOD
DANCES WITH EVIL

Bobby and I were married on a Saturday and left on Monday morning to play in a fall league for professional baseball players. We lived in an apartment above a garage, and each day Bobby would go to practice while I would twiddle my thumbs. I begged God to fill my time with meaningful things, and since this was the first time in my life I didn't have a Day-Timer overflowing with work and activities, I was eager to see what he would do.

I stopped every day at the local 7-Eleven to refill my soda cup before going to Bobby's games, and every time I pulled into the parking lot, I saw a desolate-looking man sitting in front of the store. He was filthy and spoke with a lisp as he described his painful life to me, and like a child finding a lost puppy, I developed a friendship with him immediately. A newlywed, and a bit bored, I began to make food to take to my new friend, whose name was Bill.

One day he explained he was trying to get a driver's license so he could get a job; the only trouble was that he struggled to read. Reading was my specialty in college, so with the idea of being a Mother Teresa, I assured him I could help. He gave me his house address, and I agreed to meet him there later that night to help him study for the test.

Bobby wasn't as compassionate toward Bill as I was. As a matter of fact, he was downright skeptical, which annoyed me as I tried to explain the sweet intent of my friend from 7-Eleven. We finally agreed he would go with me to Bill's house, a caution I thought was completely ridiculous.

When we got there, we were stunned by the filth and chaos of his one-room dwelling. He had nowhere for me to sit but on the side of his bed, where he promptly plopped down beside me. Bobby stood by the door as I nervously asked for the driver's manual. There was no driver's manual, and my filthy friend suddenly lunged in for a kiss! Bobby quickly ushered me out the door, and by the time we got home, I was shaking in disbelief.

"I thought he was so nice!" I repeated over and over.

Bobby looked me square in the eyes and said, "Not everyone's nice, Gari. Some people have evil intent." Although I was protected that night from what could have been a disaster, I've never forgotten that evil dances where good lives. If we don't learn to stand, it will rob us, maim us, and spit in the face of our unsuspecting hearts.

Every believer will come face-to-face with evil at some point in their lives — not just the kind that brags in scary headlines or the crawl at the bottom of a news show, but an evil that requires a reaction or response. What is our response to things that scare us? What do we do when evil spits in our face?

In 1994, Rwandan native Immaculée Ilibagiza was twenty-two years old and home from college to spend Easter with her devout Catholic family when the death of Rwanda's Hutu president sparked a three-month slaughter of nearly one million ethnic Tutsis. She survived by hiding in a Hutu pastor's tiny bathroom with seven other starving women for ninety-one cramped, terrifying days. Ilibagiza describes the scene from the tiny bathroom window as she looked out at those ravenously fed by hatred and bloodshed:

> It was my turn to stretch when a commotion erupted outside. There were dozens, maybe hundreds of voices, some yelling, others chanting. We knew immediately that the killers had arrived.

"Let us hunt them in the forests, lakes, and hills; let us find them in the church; let us wipe them from the face of the earth!"

I stood on my tiptoes and peeked out the window through a little hole in the curtain. The other ladies grabbed at me, trying to pull me down ...

I ignored them, knocking their hands away and peering through the hole. I immediately regretted my decision because I was petrified by what I saw.

Hundreds of people surrounded the house, many of whom were dressed like devils, wearing skirts of tree bark and shirts of dried banana leaves, and some even had goat horns strapped onto their heads. Despite their demonic costumes, their faces were easily recognizable, and there was murder in their eyes.

They whooped and hollered. They jumped about, waving spears, machetes, and knives in the air. They chanted a chilling song of genocide while doing a dance of death ...

It wasn't the soldiers who were chanting, nor was it the trained militiamen who had been tormenting us for days. No, these were my neighbors, people I'd grown up and gone to school with — some had even been to our house for dinner.[25]

How do you reconcile the sight of friends, teachers, and community leaders circling homes as they scream for the blood of their neighbors? It makes no sense, and yet evil rarely does. Murder, corruption, kidnapping, and abuse are saturated with evil's stench.

The apostle Paul instructs, "Overcome evil with good" (Romans 12:21); John states, "You have overcome the evil one" (1 John 2:13); and Jesus asks the Father to "deliver us from the evil one" (Matthew 6:13). But why is it tempting to look away, to pretend that evil won't circle *our* house and make *us* quiver?

In the year 605 BC, evil was stirring when a man named Nebuchadnezzar became king of Babylon. Babylon was a huge empire to the east of the Jewish nation of Judah, and Nebuchadnezzar wanted to weaken Judah and take over its territory, which he accomplished by seizing its holy city, Jerusalem. He didn't just attack Jerusalem; he destroyed it, taking the best-looking, brightest men and women back to Babylon to assimilate them into his kingdom.

Daniel and his three friends — Shadrach, Meshach, and Abednego (Babylonian names given to them after they arrived) — were probably about fifteen or sixteen years old when their country was attacked. They were kidnapped and forced to travel back to Babylon to serve in the king's training program. Immediately these young Jewish men vowed to honor God, so they refused to eat the king's delicacies and drink the royal wine and asked for only vegetables and water instead.

When the three-year training period was complete, these four men passed with brilliant colors. They were smarter than the other men and held in high esteem by King Nebuchadnezzar himself. It seemed they were able to *stand up* for God (eating veggies and remaining true to their convictions) without having to *stand out*. It's a bit like coworkers who know you go to church and see you wearing a cross around your neck; they accept you and may actually give a nod of approval. But when you speak out against policies that lean toward cheating or personally withdraw from actions or conversations that hurt other people, now you've set yourself apart — and you may have to face an upturned nose or someone saying, "Who does she think she is?"

Shadrach, Meshach, and Abednego knew who they were, but with a vile evil stirring around them, they were about to move from standing up to standing out as their faith endured the threat of annihilation.

Forced to Take a Stand

It's one thing to battle evil from the confines of an ideology, a political party, or a committee, but it's quite another to take a stand on your own two feet. This is what happened to these eighteen-year-old men when King Nebuchadnezzar made an image of gold he required everyone to bow to. The image was as tall as a nine-foot building and could easily be seen throughout the kingdom since it was built on the plain of Dura. Whenever the distinct sounds of the royal orchestra wafted through the air, the entire kingdom had to fall down to worship — and it wasn't optional.

> Then the herald loudly proclaimed, "Nations and peoples of every language, this is what you are commanded to do: As soon as you hear the sound of the horn, flute, zither, lyre, harp, pipe and all kinds of music, you must fall down and worship the image of gold that King Nebuchadnezzar has set up. Whoever does not fall down and worship will immediately be thrown into a blazing furnace."
>
> DANIEL 3:4 – 6

I believe there are three stages to battling evil, and every person who has ever taken a stand against its fiery grip has had to work through them. First is the stage of *disbelief* — the stage where you can't believe something so horrible is actually happening. You're shocked and surprised, as if you've been watching a scene from a movie rather than something real that is unfolding before you.

I grew up in a quaint Colorado suburb outside of Denver. Snuggled in the shadow of the Rocky Mountains, we lived in a community called Applewood Knolls, and the streets and houses were as well kept and charming as the name would indicate. The kids in our neighborhood loved kickball, late night hide-and-seek games, and swimming at the local pool — so you can imagine our terror when a murder took place at the end of our quaint block.

I often babysat for the family at the end of our street. They had three adorable kids, and although we heard rumors the husband was involved with the Mafia, we laughed about the possibility and considered it nothing more than "movie-type" drama. Late one night, as the husband returned home, a man with a gun crouched behind the bricks of their front porch and shot him dead as he reached for the front door. For weeks, people drove up and down our cul-de-sac to take a look at the house of the gunned-down Mafia man. I couldn't get out of my head the images of this daddy lying on his front porch. We were in disbelief that something so tragic and criminal could happen on our sweet little street — but it did.

Shadrach, Meshach, and Abednego must have been in disbelief when they heard about the golden image on the plain of Dura. I can just hear them saying to one another, "I thought losing our homes, being kidnapped from our families, and forced into the king's service was bad enough, and now we're threatened with death if we don't bow down to worship a false god! Can it get any worse?"

Have you ever asked that question only to find out, yes, things *can* get worse? A doctor's diagnosis, a financial struggle, a strained relationship, tough deadlines — sometimes it feels like we're wandering in a bleak tunnel with only the glow of a match to light the way. Just when you think it can't get any worse, the match burns out and you're left in complete darkness. It's in these times that the light of Jesus can lead us to new openings or fresh perspective. When our matches burn out, we need him to light a new fire and carry us to safety and rest.

For a while, our boys were able to refuse to acknowledge the false image and remain unnoticed. When the music played, they didn't bow — and no one seemed to care. But soon a group of astrologers known for their fortune-telling practices came forward and brought charges against the Jews. These astrologers may well have been jealous of the young Jews' position in the king's court, so they used tattling to try to get rid of them.

> At this time some astrologers came forward and denounced the Jews. They said to King Nebuchadnezzar, "May the king live forever! Your Majesty has issued a decree ... But there are some Jews whom you have set over the affairs of the province of Babylon — Shadrach, Meshach and Abednego — who pay no attention to you, Your Majesty. They neither serve your gods nor worship the image of gold you have set up."
>
> DANIEL 3:8 – 10, 12

This tattle sent the king into a wild rage as he brought the three men before him for questioning. Up until now their customs and faith had been relatively safe, hidden away in a spiritual safe deposit box that few had access to. But now that the box had been opened, everyone would see its contents, and the king would be forced to face the staunch verdict he had imposed.

DEALING WITH RAGE

King Nebuchadnezzar erupted. Have you ever tried to reason with a person like this? Raging people's agenda usually sounds like this:

- Follow me! Do as I say.
- I'm in charge — so don't question me.
- Don't expose me; if you do, I'll hurt you.
- Feed my insecurities. Tell me what I want to hear and submit to my authority.

Dealing with raging people can be dangerous and exhausting, and I'm always surprised by the varied complexions of people who rage. It's not just big, powerful men who seethe with fury; sometimes quiet women are raging as they utter comments that slice through innocent hearts and shatter hope.

It's interesting how rage can simmer under the surface of certain personalities, and the slightest temperature increase or change of plans can blow the top right off their pot. My friend Andrea faced the rage of a man and woman who were cloaked in good but functioned in evil. During a college internship in Uganda, she uncovered an evil so great that it could make the hair on your arms stand up.

A "Christian" couple was running an orphanage ironically named Maranatha, which means "the Lord is coming." When Andrea, her sister Leah, and a friend named Sally traveled to Uganda, the Lord *did* come in the form of these caring young women — and through them an evil plot was uncovered.

Andrea recalls seeing 162 children living at the orphanage "in the worst conditions imaginable. These kids, aged four to fourteen, were sleeping in three tiny rooms without beds or blankets on a rocky dirt floor. Rats climbed over them as they slept, and their bedrooms turned to mud when it rained. Their bodies were covered in rashes, and many suffered from bacterial infections from the unsanitary latrines. During the day, they would fight over a spot in the long line to receive their one meal a day that only teased their empty bellies."[26] The building that housed them was on an alley, which made them even more vulnerable. Girls were hired out for sex and were raped, while others became thieves in order to survive.

Even more disturbing was the fact that this couple had turned their orphanage into a lucrative business. They would take pictures of the starving kids and receive donations and support, but none of the money went toward the kids; instead it went toward their profit.

When it came time for the girls to return to the United States, they experienced a watershed moment so intense that it changed the course of their lives forever. Andrea decided to stay and overcome the evil, while Leah and Sally returned home to try to raise funds to help. Nothing could prepare Andrea for the months that lay ahead as she stared evil in the face every single day.

First, she exposed the couple running Maranatha and the travesty of this fake refuge for kids. She proposed to the authorities a new orphanage that she would run with the help of a few local Ugandans. They reluctantly agreed she could take half of the children, but that was only the beginning of her battle against evil.

Once they settled into their new home — a plot of land with buildings they later transformed into a school, a church, and a fish pond — evil took an even darker plunge. Over the course of their first six months together, almost nightly, Andrea and her Ugandan friends went face-to-face with the Devil. Children would fall into seizures; they would scream and cry out as their eyes rolled to the back of their sockets. One brother even tried to kill his sister while overcome by an evil stupor.

Andrea described these events to me on my first visit to the orphanage as we worked in a supply room in the back of the facility. I was stunned by the poise of her bold belief. She explained that when these things happened (almost always in the dead of night), they would gather all the children out on the field in front of the school and make a circle, where they would loudly repeat the same lines over and over, covering the children in prayer: *You belong to Jesus. Jesus loves you. You are his.*

This was the stuff of horror movies, and now she was living it each night. She was delivering children from the Evil One, just as Jesus prayed in his prayer to the Father (Matthew 6:9 – 13).

After six intense months of head-to-head confrontation, peace began to settle over her new orphanage, appropriately named Musana, which means sunshine (or as they say "Sonshine"). Andrea had moved from the first stage of battling evil — *disbelief* — to the next stage, where evil's power is upended — *settled belief.*

Settled belief is digging in and saying, "I won't let fear or frustration thwart the good that God can bring from wicked intent. I won't be shaken or moved." It's in these startling moments that a watershed of overcoming evil takes place. When we bravely look evil in the eye and say, "Stand down!" we learn to stand up.

Have you ever found yourself trying to figure out how lives get so messed up? How it's possible for people to fall into such dark recesses in their minds? Although we may not be battling evil in Africa, we do face darkness in our neighborhoods, our schools, our workplaces, and our families. It's helpful to know that the slope toward evil always begins with temptation, and Satan hasn't come up with any new material in this department. He's still using the same techniques he used on Adam, Eve, and Jesus.

Rick Warren notes that temptation follows a four-step process that is replayed time and again throughout the Bible:

> In step one, Satan identifies a *desire* inside of you. It may be a sinful desire, like the desire to get revenge or to control others, or it may be a legitimate desire, like the desire to be loved and valued or to feel pleasure ...

We think temptation lies around us, but God says it begins *within* us. If you didn't have the internal desire, the temptation could not attract you. Temptation always starts in your mind, not in circumstances.[27]

The second step in this four-step process is *doubt.* Doubting God's goodness or his good intent can easily lead to temptation. In the garden, Satan whispered to Eve, "You won't die! God knows you'll be more like him if you eat from this tree!" Suddenly Eve was confused about God. *Why would he hold out on us? Why wouldn't he want us to be more like him?* She doubted his goodness, thereby opening herself up to the taunt of temptation.

The third step is *deception*, that vulnerable place where we think we can get away with something we sense deep down isn't right. It's here that we dole out excuses such as, "I'm not as bad as everyone else" or "No one will ever know; it's no big deal."

The final step is *disobedience* — that point when we cross the line and act on what has been vying for our attention. We willfully make a choice to disobey, and what started as a playful distraction has now become a dangerous liaison.

Through the lens of these steps, it's easy to see how people end up in the pit of sin and bad choices. If disobedience is rewarded or encouraged, it gives way to all sorts of evil. This is how the couple who ran the orphanage ended up so corrupt. It's how husbands end up in the beds of women who aren't their wives, and how abusers rationalize forcing themselves on their prey. It's also where King Nebuchadnezzar found himself as he raged at the young boys he had kidnapped and forced into submission. Sooner or later, evil gets exposed, and when it does, it takes the settled belief of people like Shadrach, Meshach, and Abednego to topple it.

13

MATURITY'S PRIZE — SURRENDER

If disbelief is the gateway to acknowledging evil, settled belief is where we put on our boots and kick. It's making the decision to enter the brawl, regardless of what happens or what the personal outcome may be. When Shadrach, Meshach, and Abednego watched the king's furious reaction to their refusal to bow to his god, they responded with settled belief. No matter what threats he screamed or what facial expressions he flaunted, they responded with calm resolve.

> Shadrach, Meshach and Abednego replied to him, "King Nebuchadnezzar, we do not need to defend ourselves before you in this matter. If we are thrown into the blazing furnace, the God we serve is able to deliver us from it, and he will deliver us from Your Majesty's hand. *But even if he does not*, we want you to know, Your Majesty, that we will not serve your gods or worship the image of gold you have set up."
>
> DANIEL 3:16 – 18, italics mine

In the face of fury, these three young men utter some of the most powerful words in the Bible. They say, "Our God can deliver us — but even if he chooses not to, he's still God!" Only those who have entered into settled belief have the courage and maturity to make a statement like that—and then risk their lives for its truth. This is their moment, their watershed, that overcomes that which has tried to overcome them.

When you come to this point in your faith, you're on your way to the golden prize of maturity—surrender. This type of surrender isn't weak, and it's definitely not a fatalistic throwing in the towel. On the contrary, this surrender is the same strength that carried Jesus to the cross. At any moment he could have called down legions of angels to destroy his persecutors, but instead he surrendered to the splinters of wood and the pounding of nails. "He's still God, even if he lets me die" was Jesus' creed as he moaned on the cross, and these young men understood the power of this type of release. Surrender says, "I can't control the situation, but I love and trust the God who can. The outcome of this circumstance doesn't change the God I love."

When you're facing a burning furnace, it is certainly tempting to jump ship and run toward excuses, but excuses are the archenemy of surrender. Excuses will snuff out surrender faster than the extinguishing of a candle burning in the rain.

What if Shadrach, Meshach, and Abednego had collapsed under the pressure of excuses? What if they had caved under the breath of fear? Their excuses may have sounded something like this:

- We will bow down but not actually *worship* the idol.
- We won't become idol worshipers, but we'll do this one time, then ask God for forgiveness.
- The king has absolute power and we must obey him. God will understand.
- The king appointed us—we owe this to him.
- This is a foreign land, so God will excuse us for following the customs of this land.
- Our ancestors set up idols in God's temple! This isn't half as bad!
- We're not hurting anybody.
- If we get ourselves killed and some heathens take our high positions, they won't help our people in exile![28]

Any of these excuses could have derailed our heroes, including one we all have to watch out for: "God will understand this is too much pressure. I have no choice but to conform." Excuses and conforming are rivals to faith; but when we're committed to settled belief, they look like ridiculous substitutes for what we love most — honoring God.

FROM FLAMES TO GLORY

To say that King Nebuchadnezzar was insulted by the settled belief of these three young men is an understatement. He was so angry that he made his servants heat up the furnace seven times hotter than usual and called in the strongest men in his army to tie them up and throw them into the flames. Fully clothed, and with ropes dangling from their hands and feet, Shadrach, Meshach, and Abednego were pushed into the flames. The furnace was so hot that it devoured the soldiers who had thrown them in!

Notice what happened next:

> But suddenly, as he was watching, Nebuchadnezzar jumped up in amazement and exclaimed to his advisors, "Didn't we throw three men into the furnace?"
>
> "Yes," they said, "we did indeed, Your Majesty."
>
> "Well, look!" Nebuchadnezzar shouted. "I see *four* men, unbound, walking around in the fire, and they aren't even hurt by the flames! And the fourth looks like a god!"
>
> DANIEL 3:24 – 25 LB

Nebuchadnezzar is about to lose his mind. He can't believe what his eyes are seeing. First of all, his guards have been burned to death as they pushed these men into the flames. Then the ropes that bound his prisoners were unfastened, and now they are sauntering around the flames talking to someone who's definitely not human. That's a lot to take in, especially when you think you know it all.

Some scholars think the heavenly being in the flames was an angel, while others think it was a pre-incarnate appearance of Christ — either way, Shadrach, Meshach, and Abednego are walking in the midst of a miracle. I often wonder what they talked about in the fire. Were they giddy with excitement or reverent in awe? I know if I were walking around in flames with Jesus or an angel strolling next to me, I'd be shouting praise at the top of my lungs!

What happened next is what I call "God's boomerang effect." It's often in the midst of hardship and evil that miracles are born. What was thrown out as evil comes back a miracle.

Nebuchadnezzar's reaction to what he's seen is stunning. He's witnessed something so miraculous that he begins to change from idol worshiper to servant of the Most High God.

> Nebuchadnezzar then approached the opening of the blazing furnace and shouted, "Shadrach, Meshach and Abednego, servants of the Most High God, come out! Come here!"
>
> So Shadrach, Meshach and Abednego came out of the fire, and the satraps, prefects, governors and royal advisers crowded around them. They saw that the fire had not harmed their bodies, nor was a hair of their heads singed; their robes were not scorched, and there was no smell of fire on them.
>
> Then Nebuchadnezzar said, "Praise be to the God of Shadrach, Meshach and Abednego, who has sent his angel and rescued his servants! They trusted in him and defied the king's command and were willing to give up their lives rather than serve or worship any god except their own God."
>
> DANIEL 3:26 – 28

Miracles start with an awakening, a stirring, an expectant hope that awaits intervention. Without an awakening, we're often not even aware that something spectacular is taking place. Nebuchadnezzar certainly wasn't expecting a miracle; he was ushering in death — but God turned the events meant for harm into an awakening, and every awakening is a miracle. This awakening belonged to the king, and from this point on, God would shake him, break him, and remake him into a humble king fixed on God's glory.

Shadrach, Meshach, and Abednego began with *disbelief* as they looked at the cruel circumstances that defined their lives. They moved to *settled belief* when they chose to stand against the evil, no matter the cost. Then they entered the final stage in battling evil, a stage that is fresh and surprising when you've been knocked down by evil's blows — *new belief*. Ironically, out of the ashes of heartache comes the beauty of new belief.

One of the greatest scenes of pure evil I've witnessed was the massacre at Columbine High School. I taught at an elementary school that was a ten-minute drive from Columbine, and although my school was housed in a different district, we were neighbors. My classroom was situated next to our school's office, and at midday I began to sense something was wrong. The office staff was scrambling to find a TV (this was before smartphones and YouTube videos) so they could catch up with what was being relayed to local school principals. All we knew was that a shooting was in progress at a school near ours — and the situation was devastating at best.

On April 20, 1999, two high school seniors carried out a massacre at the high school in the middle of the day. The boys' plan was to kill hundreds of their peers with guns, knives, and a multitude of bombs. When the day was done, twelve students, one teacher, and two murderers were dead, and twenty-one people were injured. If we picture evil with legs, it walked through the halls of Columbine High School that day.

After we cautiously dismissed the last of our elementary students, I rushed home to sit in front of the TV and try to make sense of this tragedy unfolding on hallowed ground — a school building. One of the teachers I worked with had a son who attended Columbine. She tearfully recalled how he was running toward a staircase to escape when a teacher pushed himself in front of her son as a shield of protection. Moments later, that teacher was struck by a bullet, a bullet that would have struck her son if the teacher hadn't stood in his place. Another boy recalls climbing into the roof rafters to hide as he was abandoned by everyone else in the room; he was terrified to move out into the hallways, where evil was having a free-for-all binge of devastation.

The day after the shooting, I was walking around our playground on recess duty when a car driving by the fence backfired. Thinking I was hearing gunshots, I started to run to gather as many kids as I could — knowing I could only protect a handful from bullets meant to kill. When I realized what had happened, I collapsed in a heap on the ground, inconsolable as I wept over this senseless tragedy.

The following weekend, Bobby and I took our three children to a hill behind the high school where an interesting phenomenon was taking place. A man from the Chicago area had built thirteen large crosses and placed them at the top of the lonely hill. The hill became a pilgrimage spot for mourners seeking a place to pour out their anguish. Climbing that hill was cathartic, and for months people met there to pray, to cry, and to hold one another.

Another movement began as the teens of the city banded together in a holy cluster of grace. People of all denominations could be seen praying with others, reading Scripture, and stepping in to help with the pain that seemed to ooze from the city's streets and corridors. Homes were opened for Bible studies, prayer groups gathered, and adults stepped in to mentor teens, while teens mentored one another.

Out of the worst kind of tragedy, we experienced a watershed moment. It started like a small hush, the kind you can't even acknowledge when you're weighed down with anger and grief. But soon the fellowship of sorrow gave way to light, and new belief began to blossom like the buds of spring. This must be what Paul meant when he wrote, "Do not be overcome by evil, but overcome evil with good" (Romans 12:21). It's the tender moment when you realize that what was meant to harm you has actually strengthened you. Out of the ashes comes new belief.

Part Seven

THE WATERSHED
OF BELIEF

14

GOD-MOVEMENTS

I love feeling like I'm part of something important. Most of my life I've been a "rally girl," drawing people toward a purpose or making them feel like they're part of a bigger team. When I was a teacher, my third graders' eyes would grow wide as we read stories about the plight of the disadvantaged, about children suffering in Africa or on another continent. "We need to *do* something, Mrs. Meacham!" they'd lament. And I'd shake my head and reply, "You're right; we do."

One year, this type of exchange led to a full-scale assault. I gathered my class around my stool and asked them what they thought we should do. Ideas were flying as I captured their thoughts on chart paper. "Give kids in Africa money for food." "Help them to be healthy and safe." "What about water? Let's give them water!"

In my bravest adult voice (the one grown-ups use when they know kids are dreaming a bit out of their league), I asked, "And what can we do to help make these ideas happen?" My class started sharing ideas as fast as I could write them — a garage sale, a bake sale, and a school-wide campaign to collect donations.

What I saw transpire over the next two months was stunning. I showed my class a catalog from an organization committed to providing for the needy throughout the world. We went through it page by page, earmarking the items that caught our eye and then voting on our top picks. When the list was done we had our goals — food packages for children in an impoverished village, backpacks filled with school supplies, a goat for a family, and a wheelchair for a child with a disability (they threw that one in because they knew my daddy was in a wheelchair and it always made them sad).

I wish I could say I was hopeful we'd meet our goals, but truthfully, it seemed like Peter Pan would really fly before we'd be able to put together the kind of money we needed to supply all the things my class wanted to provide. So with the resolve of an A-list actress, I pretended to have faith that we would raise the money we needed.

We started with a garage sale on a Saturday morning. Families brought old toys, clothing, and furniture, while classmates took turns working at the sale. We made around two hundred dollars that day, which I was thankful for, but it was nowhere near what we needed to reach our goals. The kids were elated and kept saying, "Mrs. Meacham, we're getting close!"

For the next few weeks, faithful moms would bake all kinds of goodies and bring them to school to be purchased at lunchtime. Cookies and brownies for fifty cents weren't catapulting us to large coffers, but we were steady and hopeful. Daily I had to hide my tears as I watched my students bring in birthday money, money they had saved for toys, or money they earned after asking their parents to give them work to do around the house. Our "money can" (a used coffee can the kids had decorated in bright African colors) was starting to get a bit heavy. Bobby and I promised to double whatever we made, and parents and teachers from around the building began writing checks to increase our funds.

One week before our efforts were scheduled to end, I received a letter from the organization that was going to receive our gift. It stated that a United States grant had been awarded to the organization — for the next two months any donation received would be matched six times the amount! Our class erupted in whoops, jumps, and some tears after that news. We were later notified that our donation fed an entire village for six months — along with the backpacks, goat, and wheelchair. We had lavishly outrun our goals! A movement was sparked by the compassion of children and a coffee can of hope.

Every "movement" starts with an idea and progresses from there. It's funny how the word *movement* begins with the word *move*. You won't have a movement if people don't move, and you won't experience a movement of God if God doesn't move. A God-movement is evident when circumstances and faith intersect. There's no explanation as to how things are playing out other than "God is on the move."

One of the most striking God-movements recorded in the Bible took place after the Israelites had roamed the wilderness for forty years. Although this generation witnessed the parting of the sea in their departure from Egyptian slavery and oppression, they still couldn't wrap their minds around who this God was.

Even so, it annoys me greatly when people write the Israelites off as if their wandering years were a complete waste. It was during this time that a new generation learned to trust God. Children watched their parents gather manna each day, trusting that tomorrow more food would be provided. They watched their mothers, fathers, and relatives relocate from place to place in a brave, nomadic lifestyle. Because of their unfaithfulness when the journey began, the generation that marched out of Egypt wasn't allowed to enter the Promised Land, but there's no denying they raised up kids who were eager to receive the promise. If they hadn't, nobody would have budged when God was ready for his movement to take shape.

PHASES OF A GOD-MOVEMENT

In the world, a movement starts with a need that people understand, followed by a call to an action they can join. In God's kingdom, a movement starts with a need, followed by a humble breaking of our will — so that the call to action is his, not ours.

After forty years of drifting, the time had come for the new generation of Israelites to claim their stake. With the strength of his mentor

Moses, Joshua told the people to purify themselves. " 'For tomorrow,' " he said, 'the Lord will do a great miracle' " (Joshua 3:5 LB).

The next morning, Joshua ordered the priests to take the ark of the covenant and cross the full-flowing Jordan River. At that time of year, the Jordan was impossible to cross without being exposed to the danger of drowning or being swept away. As millions of Israelites followed the ark, the river swirled and stood like a mighty wall to one side so God's people could cross in complete safety.

Although this scene could bring a movie crowd to their feet in applause, what intrigues me is what happens next. It's unexpected and unscripted as Joshua turns a celebration into a time of sober reflection. Once the people crossed the Jordan, they camped on the eastern edge of Jericho in a place called Gilgal. It's here that God told them to make sharp knives and cut themselves through the rite of circumcision. After a time of great anticipation and hype, God wants his people to be cut. Most God-movements, in fact, have three things in common: a time of *cutting*, a time of *healing*, and a time of *conquering*. In this new land of promise, the first thing God does is allow pain.

Circumcision means "to cut around." Most of us are familiar with the act of circumcision when a male child is born. It's a routine procedure often performed for hygienic reasons, but in Joshua's day, circumcision was performed for spiritual reasons. A study note in the *Life Application Bible* states, "When God made the original covenant with Abraham, he required that each male be circumcised as a sign of cutting off the old life and beginning a new life with God ... Other cultures at that time used circumcision as a sign of entry into adulthood, but only Israel used it as a sign of following God."[29]

The Israelites who came out of Egypt had all been circumcised, but the males born in the wilderness had not. Although I'm not a male and I'm not Jewish, and I live centuries after this covenant took place, as a woman I've wondered, "What about *us*, God?" How do women reflect this *cutting off* that a man's body was assured of? I was delighted to hear the words spoken by Moses to both men and women shortly before he died: "The LORD your God will *circumcise your heart* and the heart of your descendants, to love the LORD your God with all your heart and with all your soul, so that you may live" (Deuteronomy 30:6 NASB, italics mine).

A physical circumcision reminds us to be set apart, while a heart circumcision cuts off anything that keeps us from doing so. In this way, both men and women are meant to have incisions on their hearts, places where God has sliced away anything that blocks the flow of his love, grace, and purpose. Why does God cut? Why do we writhe, question, and cry out in pain? Why does he insist that we be set apart?

Dwight L. Moody has been called the most famous and effective evangelist for Christ in the nineteenth century, but before reaching his potential in preaching, he was cut for greater glory. Although Dwight was poorly educated, he was in love with God, and shortly after moving to Chicago, the class he taught on Sundays to young people grew to over a thousand students. Though he appeared to be thriving, something inside of him kept gnawing at him, refusing to let go. He sensed he was supposed to leave Chicago to become a traveling evangelist — but whenever he thought about this lifestyle, he said "no way" to God.

On October 8, 1871, Moody spoke to his Sunday school listeners, asking them to come back the following Sunday prepared to make a decision to respond to Christ, but they never got that chance. As services ended, fire alarms sounded in the streets. The meeting ended in a state of panic, and the young people left the building to find the city in terror. Flames leaped into the sky, swallowing whole buildings. Gas mains were exploding, and the streets became clogged with fleeing people. The Great Chicago Fire burned from Sunday to Wednesday, and Moody lost both his church building and his home.[30]

Deeply shaken, Moody quickly left Chicago for New York in the hope that he could rebuild his scorched life. While walking down Wall Street, Moody experienced a watershed moment — a moment so powerful that he rarely spoke of it, calling it a sacred experience beyond what words could express. "I cried all the time, begging God to fill me with His Spirit, when suddenly God showed up as I walked the streets of New York."[31]

It wasn't in a physical appearance that God showed himself, but rather in a moment of clarity and truth. Moody's pain and confusion now made sense — the fires, the loss, the unsettled wandering — and it was through this watershed moment that Moody agreed to go wherever God would take him. Set apart for a God-movement, he was ready to move — but only after a season of pain.

If you're in a season of pain — the loss of a loved one, loss of a job, loss of a relationship, loss of identity, loss of hope — know that God is preparing you for his glory through it. We can't understand God's glory unless we've struggled through pain. In discomfort, we feel the caress of Christ, and within that caress is the balm of a watershed moment — a moment in which we have yielded to pain so God can heal us for a higher purpose.

Although some seasons of pain have nothing to do with our choices, God will sometimes have to cut away tissue that is choking his power in our lives. One of these cuts is *sin*. So often women beg God for answers to the same prayers, but sin is tying his hands from blessing. I recently spoke to a beautiful young woman who attends church regularly and goes to Bible study. Her fervent desire is to marry a godly man and have a family. Yet she sleeps with anyone she dates and recently moved in with her current boyfriend. For her to move forward in a God-movement, she'll have to allow God to cut through her insecure inclination to give herself away.

It's encouraging to see that many people in the Bible needed to have sin cut out of their lives. Moses saw an Egyptian guard beating a Hebrew man, so he murdered him and buried him in the sand. God had to cut out Moses' sin during the time he fled to Midian, and it was there that Moses was healed and trained to be the leader of a nation. Paul hated Christians, and on his way to destroy them, he was struck by Jesus. Blind for three days, it was after his sin was cut out that he received true sight. Sin gets in the way of glory, and a wise man or woman will let God cut it away.

Indifference also requires cutting. You can't be set apart *and* blend in. To be indifferent is to not care about how God feels about things. It boils down to shaping God in our image rather than acknowledging that we're made in his. Surfing the waves of cultural opinion and public approval may be manageable for a while, but eventually this wave will hit the beach, and we'll be left with nothing more than a surfboard and a tan. You can't claim God's movement in your life without agreeing to his terms.

The last thing God cuts away is *flawed thinking*. This one is tricky, because many of us have been duped for a long time. When I was young, I was told by a church authority that I couldn't read the Bible on my own because I didn't have the skills to interpret it. I was actually afraid to open it, even though I kept one on my nightstand beside my bed! I was tricked into thinking it was beyond my skill set to understand, and I wasted years believing the Bible was irrelevant.

Flawed thinking can dictate the choices we make and our responses to life's options. Think about the woman Jesus spoke to at the well in Samaria. When Jesus offered her living water that would quench beyond the scope of physical refreshment, she responded straight from her flawed religious perspective: "Are you greater than our father Jacob, who gave us the well and drank from it himself, as did also his sons and his livestock?" (John 4:12).

This woman spoke not from a love for Jacob, a forefather of the Jewish faith, but from a religious wink — much like people who wear crosses as jewelry or on clothes but don't care about their meaning. When Jesus tried to explain that *he* is the well of water springing up to eternal life, the woman's flawed thinking kept her in the shallow puddles of faith. "Sir, give me this water so that I won't get thirsty and have to keep coming here to draw water" (John 4:15).

When Jesus instructed her to summon her husband and come back, she told him she didn't have a husband. And Jesus replied, "You are right when you say you have no husband. The fact is, you have had five husbands, and the man you now have is not your husband. What you have just said is quite true" (John 4:17 – 18).

In two sharp sentences, Jesus circumcised her sin. He took the flint knife of truth and cut away at what kept her flawed. Immediately, this woman tried to change the subject by bringing up more religious mumbo jumbo: "I know that Messiah" (called Christ) "is coming. When he comes, he will explain everything to us" (John 4:25). But Jesus wouldn't have it. He was cutting her for her own good and pointing to her need for a Savior: "Then Jesus declared, 'I, the one speaking to you — I am he'" (John 4:26).

The woman with five husbands is in the midst of a watershed moment. From that time on, she is never the same. Her flawed thinking is replaced with sound faith as she spreads the news of the Messiah to the people in her city, ironically starting with the men.

> So the woman left her waterpot, and went into the city and said to *the men*, "Come, see a man who told me all the things that I have done; this is not the Christ, is it?" ...
>
> From that city many of the Samaritans believed in Him because of the word of the woman who testified, "He told me all the things that I have done."
>
> JOHN 4:28 – 29, 39 NASB, italics mine

This brazen woman allowed her flawed thinking to be cut away so new faith could emerge. It's remarkable that Jesus knows the precise way to cut off what threatens to keep us from his mercy. Those of us who've endured the skillful prunes of our Savior understand that without his scalpel, we are a muddled mess.

A PLACE TO HEAL

The Hebrew word *gilgal* means "roll" (Joshua 5:9), and when you're camped in pain, there's nothing better than hearing it will be rolled away. After the Israelites were cut in circumcision, God provided a place for them to heal. Gilgal was their healing place. Scripture states, "And after the whole nation had been circumcised, they remained where they were in camp until they were healed" (Joshua 5:8).

As I was growing up, my family seemed to face one problem after another. Medical problems, financial problems, and alcohol-related problems slammed us against the wall, but God provided my siblings and me a place to heal — our grandparents' homes.

One set of grandparents lived in Maryland, so each summer we'd board a plane for the East Coast. I can still smell their house, a fresh mixture of my grandmother's Oil of Olay products and the Pine-Sol she used to scrub everything clean. My grandfather was so friendly that wherever we went, people knew him — and even if they didn't, he cracked jokes and made them laugh.

They bought each of us our own bikes, and we'd get on those bikes and explore like Lewis and Clark. Their neighborhood was unchartered territory waiting to be discovered. But the best part of our time together was the week they'd take us to the beach. We'd load Grandpa's old white Ford and travel over the Chesapeake Bay Bridge to our favorite beach town, where I learned to love the water. My grandpa taught us to fight the waves, and his lessons transferred into the way I fought the waves in my life. Sometimes we'd tumble all the way to the shore in a tangle of foam and undertow, but Grandpa would wisely grab my shoulders and say, "Get back out here; you don't want to miss a good wave!"

Our other grandparents lived in a small town in the mountains of Colorado, about a two-hour drive from our home near Denver. We'd often spend weekends or school breaks at their house. My grandmother was a mix of adventure and stability. She was just as happy driving us up the steep slope of a mountain with the top off Grandpa's little red Jeep as she was sitting for hours playing board games. In the winter, she'd tie a rope to an inner tube and strap us to the back of her orange Chevy Blazer. We'd whirl around the track at the fairgrounds, sprawling into snowbanks as she accelerated at just the right time, sending us two feet off the tube in a hysterical bounce of laughter. I think I got my wild side from her — not wild in the sense of breaking rules, but wild with possibility, and wild for the chance to enjoy an adventurous God.

My grandparents were my Gilgal. Their love, stability, and delight in who I was became my safe place — the place that enabled me to heal from the cuts that life inflicted. If God has allowed pain in your life, he will provide a place for you to heal. Maybe this place is the safety of a good friend. Maybe it's a physical move away from things that pose a danger to you. Maybe it is a repeated reminder that you are not alone and that God is at work in the midst of boring jobs and routine days. This is your Gilgal, and from this place God will bring new life.

GROWTH IN GILGAL

As the men in the camp were healing from circumcision, Joshua invited the people to celebrate the Passover — the first to be celebrated in the Promised Land, and only the third to be celebrated by Israel since the exodus from Egypt.[32] There must have been an excited buzz in the camp as they thanked God for their healing, the privilege of being set apart as God's people, and the fresh feel of a new land of promise.

As the sun rose the following day, something remarkable happened. The manna that had been their sustenance for forty years did not appear, and it was never seen again. The only source of food this generation had known was no longer necessary as they began to eat from the gardens and grain fields in their new home. It must have felt like they were now sitting at a table in a bakery after having eaten plain tortillas for forty years! God had miraculously provided a simple form of food during the decades of wandering, and it was through this manna that they learned how to trust. But after they crossed the Jordan and endured the pain of being set apart, their lives were ready for blessing. They reconciled their time in Gilgal and came to a peaceful truce with their past. When we reconcile our pain, our sin, our wandering, we're ready to move out of Gilgal.

UNDERSTANDING YOUR GILGAL

- The pain in your life doesn't define you; God is forming a new definition *within* you.
- God provides a place to heal from the things that hurt.
- In your healing place you will grow and see new fruit begin to form.
- You won't need the old manna that used to sustain you; God is doing something new.

This new nation was experiencing a God-movement. They'd come through their season of cutting and healing — and both were necessary to prepare them for the conquering to come. Only those familiar with the cuts and bruises that set them apart are ready to conquer, and conquering proves to be the boldest watershed moment of all. It's bold because it demands belief that leaves no room for sissies. If you believe God can tear down whatever keeps you from his promised land, you're ready to march.

15

TIME
TO CONQUER

Have you ever wondered why soldiers march? Why not just walk from point A to point B? Why the structured movement of a march?

The rhythm of a march is similar to that of a chant; it induces concentration and focus and helps those marching move as quickly and fluidly as possible in one accord. Marching is a disciplined walk — intimidating to an enemy and a team builder for those who are marching. So it's interesting that when God asked the Israelites to circle the enemy city of Jericho, he told them to march.

Notice God didn't say to saunter, stroll, or meander around the city. *Marching* is a strong word, and in order to experience the watershed moments that move us from inactivity to strength, we need to march. Oswald Chambers explains God's marching orders: "I will get you out of bed, out of the languor and exhaustion, out of the state of being half dead while you are alive; I will imbue you with the spirit of life, and you will be stayed by the perfection of vital activity."[33]

The problem is I often don't understand "vital activity." How do I know the imperative activities I should join or the important movements I should become a part of? I tend to march right by them, striding toward spiritual commotion — the latest conflict, the biggest promoters, the loudest songs. There's often no sign of vital activity under these marching boots. Before I know it, instead of marching, I'm sidestepping, hip-hopping, and moving to my own silly rhythm.

I wonder if Joshua felt like sidestepping the vital task at hand, when after leading the Israelites through the Jordan River, circumcising them in Gilgal, and eating the fruit of a new land yet to be conquered, he looked at the wall of Jericho and wondered how in the world they were going to bring it down. In an earlier chapter, we talked about how Nehemiah built up a wall, but Joshua needed a wall to come down. In moments like these, God shows a strategy bigger than anything we could devise. His strategies aren't based on reality; they're based on spirituality, and Joshua was about to execute a strategy that made no sense except in the spiritual realm.

Spiritual Instructions

We're always looking for formulas — a rule, procedure, or method that promises change. But God seems to deal more freely in the area of *strategies*, which allows room to create, prepare, put together, and produce. And when God inspires a strategy for our lives, we're wise to heed it.

Joshua must have been pacing as he looked at the closed gates of Jericho within their reach. At this point, he had no idea what strategy to use for a military strike, but God was about to introduce him to someone who did.

> Now when Joshua was near Jericho, he looked up and saw a man standing in front of him with a drawn sword in his hand. Joshua went up to him and asked, "Are you for us or for our enemies?"
>
> "Neither," he replied, "but as commander of the army of the LORD I have now come." Then Joshua fell facedown to the ground in reverence, and asked him, "What message does my Lord have for his servant?"
>
> The commander of the LORD's army replied, "Take off your sandals, for the place where you are standing is holy." And Joshua did so.
>
> JOSHUA 5:13 – 15

Some moments are too holy to remain upright, and this was one of them. God was about to unfold his unconventional strategy for bringing walls down.

> Then the LORD said to Joshua, "See, I have delivered Jericho into your hands, along with its king and its fighting men. March around the city once with all the armed men. Do this for six days ... On the seventh day, march around the city seven times, with the priests blowing the trumpets. When you hear them sound a long blast on the trumpets, have the whole army give a loud shout; then the wall of the city will collapse and the army will go up, everyone straight in."
>
> JOSHUA 6:2 – 5

I can just picture the look on Joshua's face when he hears the plan to march and shout. That's it? What about weapons? What about battles? What about the way he used to fight enemies? None of that is relevant now because God is giving him a *new* strategy, and the old way of doing things no longer fits.

That tends to be our problem. We want to cling to an old way God moved, an encounter we had with him in the past, instead of watching for something new to be unveiled. When God is unveiling a strategy, it typically touches three areas that may be in need of a makeover if we're moving toward new belief: our behaviors, our hurts, and our decisions.

After years of mucking around with destructive food *behaviors* (bingeing, hiding things I ate, compulsively counting every calorie I ingested), I begged God for a new strategy. Every book I read on the topic, even Christian books, all ended the same way — with a list of recipes and a food plan to follow. I tried that strategy over and over and knew it didn't bring lasting freedom, just a white-knuckle push to try harder.

One day I read a quote from author Diane Hampton pertaining to her own struggles with food. She confessed that after reading countless diet books, undergoing self-hypnosis, and visiting a psychologist and a weight doctor, she recognized there was still something driving her to act compulsively toward food. The driving force inside her was sin.[34]

Strangely, instead of feeling condemned by the connection to food and sin, I felt hope. This was my watershed moment, a radically new way of looking at what I thought I already understood. I saw a new strategy unfolding, one that would crush my destructive behaviors with food and replace them with vibrant hope and sound thinking. In my book *Truly Fed*, I call it the "strategy of sowing seeds," and it was this God-breathed strategy that set me free.

When my friend Carrie was reprimanded at work for having a negative attitude, she was devastated. A bright and beautiful lover of God, she came face-to-face with a habit she had inherited from her mother, aunts, and grandmother. Their first reaction to anything was gloom. Worst-case scenarios were their specialty, and Carrie noticed that this morbid way of viewing life had seeped into the way she interacted not only with coworkers but with her husband and kids.

On a quest to change, Carrie had a watershed moment. She asked God for a new strategy — a new way of handling life without the gray clouds of skeptic doubt. As she prayed and listened, God showed her a pattern of belief based on the psalms and proverbs that encouraged a hopeful attitude and joyful heart in place of the flow of negative words that formerly dripped from her mouth. Within two weeks, Carrie's boss commended her for changing her attitude. She even won an award for the most promising ideas for the upcoming year! Best of all, her husband and kids savored the sweet sound of positive comments rather than the sour sounds of negative criticism and defeat.

God also gives us strategies when it comes to feelings of *hurt*. Hurt has many descriptors — pain, distress, damage, and offense — none of which are welcome guests at life's table, and yet they barge right through our front doors.

In her book *Free Yourself to Love*, my friend Jackie Kendall describes a brilliant strategy God offers for healing from hurt. It's not an easy, cookie-cutter strategy, but one that God uniquely crafts to heal our wounds and disappointments. I consider Jackie an expert on wounds, as she endured years of sexual abuse from a father who was a predator. Decades into her dynamic love for Jesus, she began to explore the very essence of the cross — forgiveness.

In her own strength she knew she couldn't offer the lottery ticket of freedom to her offender and, in turn, release the grip that shame had on her heart. But the cross taught her a different strategy, one that flies in the face of revenge, self-help, or a numbing retreat from reality. Jackie writes:

> In its most simple form, to forgive is to recognize that you have been hurt or offended, to bring the resulting hurt, anger, shock, or sadness to God, and then, by faith, to declare forgiveness. In our Christian walk, we learn to walk by faith, not by sight; I'm proposing that we forgive by faith and not by sight. Then we do it again, and again. Shampoo, rinse, repeat.
>
> I'll go into that repeating part later, but I can't emphasize enough that one of the great misconceptions about forgiveness is that it is a onetime act. The only surefire, onetime act of forgiveness was that of Jesus Christ on the cross![35]

There's a reason Jesus told Peter he would need to forgive, not just seven times for something that hurt him, but "seventy times seven" (Matthew 18:22 LB). That's 490 times and beyond, covering each time the hurt pushes its way to the forefront and tries to make itself king. God's strategy on forgiveness led Jesus to the cross and offers a new start to whomever wants it. If your life has been marred by hurt, God has a strategy to move you beyond it.

Finally, when considering God's fresh strategies, there's a pattern to how Jesus spoke to people when they needed to make *decisions* about their lives after encountering him. To the adulterous woman he said, "Go now and leave your life of sin" (John 8:11). After Jesus forgave her and offered an opportunity for a fresh start, he instructed her to stop making choices that would cycle her back to this place of embarrassment. Attention-seeking, loose behavior with men brought her to a naked point of reflection: no dark bedroom, no secret whispers — it's public now for the world to see. It's up to her as to what she'll do next, and Jesus says to "go."

I imagine her in a shameful heap on the dusty ground, aching from the blisters of rejection and ashamed to look up at the face that released her. She needs to "go" with a different attitude from the one she had when she "came." She can't stay hunched on the ground in bitter defeat. She's had a watershed moment and can no longer cower in sin, nor can she continue to make the choices that led her there. To "go" means to walk away changed, to refuse to crawl back to a bedroom retreat.

To his friend Martha, Jesus pointed out her need to overcome her worry (Luke 10:41). To the blind man he said, "Receive your sight; your faith has healed you" (Luke 18:42). Each needed a new strategy. Each needed new hope. It's when we listen to the strategies of God that we revel in a fresh watershed moment. Suddenly things make sense as we believe him and leave our former slouching to try something new.

THE GIFT OF SILENCE

Strangely, after Joshua shared God's marching strategy with the priests and armed men, he told them to be quiet: "You shall not shout nor let your voice be heard nor let a word proceed out of your mouth, until the day I tell you, 'Shout!' Then you shall shout!" (Joshua 6:10 NASB).

Why did Joshua insist on the Israelites keeping their mouths shut? As a teacher, I repeated that request more times than I care to admit. "Quiet … No talking … Silence!" Now that I've spent years studying the dynamics of human interaction, I think I know why.

We talk ourselves out of victory. When lots of voices are chatting, it's easy to forget the voice of your instructor, who has told you what you need to do to succeed.

We get distracted and lose intensity. What starts as a bold march to victory can lead to a rabbit trail of defeat. So many whispers, calls, and pulls in many directions leave us wondering what we were marching for in the first place.

We get caught up in negativity and feed on one another's fears. When you're trying to march, there's nothing worse than the nagging voice of criticism. It's a form of insecurity that has no other platform but through one's voice. People who push others down with negativity are really trying to build themselves up. Sadly, negative talk usually builds fear in those who endure its hounding.

Pastor Mark Batterson writes, "I think there are two kinds of people in the world: creators and criticizers. There are people who get out of the boat and walk on water. And there are people who sit in the boat and criticize the water walkers."[36]

In Joshua's case, there were the wall marchers, and there were those who may have sat back and criticized the march — but asking the nation to be silent during the march eliminated it all. No talking themselves out of victory. No distractions or loss of intensity. No criticism to spark fear, just a silence that builds faith and a shout that expects the wall that separates them from God's promise to fall.

I've always believed that God loves to color outside the lines. He asked Noah to build an ark before the persistent rains began; he asked Abraham to put his only son on an altar; he helped David kill a giant with nothing but a slingshot and a few small stones. It shouldn't surprise us that he told Joshua to march instead of fight, because coloring outside the lines is far more interesting than dogma, formulas, or battles that require little faith.

On the last night of our Bible study titled "Watershed," I decided to do something a bit outside the lines. After teaching on Joshua and the battle of Jericho, I summed up my thinking by stating, "Here's what I know about marching":

- You have to get up and move in order to march. You can't stay seated and march at the same time.

- To march at Jericho meant you believed that God was doing something *before* you could see it with your eyes. This is the essence of faith — "confidence in what we hope for and assurance about what we do not see" (Hebrews 11:1).
- It's often in the marching — the believing without seeing — that our faith grows.
- The result of our faith growing is walls falling!

I told my precious Bible study that all week long I had asked God one simple question: "What are our walls?" The answer he gave me was anything but simple. With pen in hand, I began to jot what I think only the eyes of heaven could see — the walls that keep so many lives imprisoned: unbelief, insecurity, shame, codependence, independence, rebellion, depression, oppression, hopelessness, confusion, anger, despair, unfair circumstances, financial burdens, relational heartache, marital pain, failing health, fear, anxiety, paralysis, laziness, distraction, guilt, dreams that seem impossible, dreams that are delayed, dreams that have changed ...

The images came to my mind faster than my hand could write. I gently asked these women, "What are your walls? What needs to come down?"

The next thing I asked was different from anything we'd ever done in our time together. I asked them to march. Inviting over a thousand people to march around a sanctuary may seem impossible, but we have a large sanctuary that's encased with a circular aisle, so I spelled out each step in this mighty undertaking.

I invited everyone to stand up and follow us (the worship leader, the women's director, and me) out onto the perimeter aisle where we'd have room to march. I then instructed the women to rise and walk in a "voice fast." Absolutely no talking, giggling, or whispering as we circled the large sanctuary in a purposeful prayer walk. Instead of seven times around, we'd go three, with the first lap's focus being "*Lord, humble me.*" Our cry was to be humbled and bent toward God's cleansing fire. The purpose wasn't to beat ourselves up in a humble boxing match, but to be refined by his holy hand of grace.

The second lap's instruction was *"Lord, help me."* Was there a request, a need, a desire that welled up in their hearts? This was the time to pray about it as we marched. I assured them that as the Israelites were marching they were surely asking for favor and specific blessings; this was our time to do the same.

The third lap had one intent: *"Lord, I praise Thee"* — taking us from "humble me" to "help me" to "praise Thee." This lap was the grateful response to the reverent laps of desire. This lap wasn't about needs or walls; it was about God's goodness and truth, about the character of a God who loves to see his people march.

Words are inadequate to describe the sight of a thousand people marching silently as they prayed. Tears flowed as the shuffle of footsteps moved around the darkened sanctuary in a rhythm of hope. We eventually marched back to where we began as the women gathered at the foot of the stage rather than returning to their seats.

I invited a trumpeter to join us, and at my signal he blasted a trill of notes to awaken our silence and open our mouths in a loud shout. "Jesus! Jesus! Jesus!" The marriage of voice and instruments joined us in a moment too holy to capture on a page. We sang, we praised, we wept, as the glory of heaven dabbed our tears with a watershed moment of belief, a belief that we could be better — could be holier — and closer to our God.

Every time I explain that night to someone I cry. Not because of the events that transpired, although they were glorious, but because of the flood of certainty I felt that there was no one greater than our God, a God who specializes in moving forward rather than making us pay for what's left behind.

So it is with expectant hearts that we anticipate our watershed moments. We look for the moments that will mark us indelibly — open our eyes — and propel us to new heights of belief.

When I was sixteen, I spent the summer at my uncle's house in

Virginia. Their home was surrounded by the wooded beauty of pine trees and lush East Coast vines layered in purple and pink hues. At night I would walk through a forested lot near their home to watch the black sky glow in tiny bursts of light. Fireflies darted back and forth like a wand spreading magic across the velvet backdrop of night. For a brief moment they'd flicker, leaving an imprint on the dusk, until another firefly shared its luminous contribution to the display of light. Watershed moments are like fireflies — a burst of understanding, a flash of surrender, a flicker of hope.

A watershed's power lies in the moments when faith and understanding collide, a personal "holy of holies" where insight flows and new faith beckons. We can't go back; we won't go back — for our watershed moments have left us forever changed.

A Note from Gari

Sweet friends,

When I finish a book, it's always bittersweet because I love spending time with you as you read. I fell in love with the word *watershed* the first time I heard it, and the more I study about life's transforming moments, the more I want to know! The notion of watershed moments — those turning points that inspire us, challenge us, stop us in our tracks, and change the course of our lives — continues to intrigue me. So with great anticipation I invite you to share your watershed moments with me. I love to stay in touch with readers and interact with you as you grow. Please drop by my website (www. garimeacham.com) or follow my blog (www.garimeacham. com/blog). I hope you know I'm praying for the watershed moments in your life that will open your eyes to the breathtaking glory of God.

Sweet blessings!
Gari

Questions for Discussion and Reflection

Chapter 1: POINTS OF NO RETURN

Turning Points

1. A watershed moment is defined as a turning point brought on by circumstances that stop us in our tracks. Like a compass, these moments move us to new ways of thinking, relating, discerning, and accepting life's challenges. Have you experienced a watershed moment that became a holy marker in your life?

2. What causes us to miss out on life's defining moments?

3. The essence of a watershed experience is looking at risk and assessing it like this: "I can be safe and ignore my desire for life-changing moments," or "I can risk comfort and listen for the melody of love to inspire me." Which choice describes you? Explain.

Chapter 2: SHIFTING PATHS

Turning Points

1. If change is an absolute in life, why do we hide from new experiences or from a truth that can set us free? Why does *what we are* look better than *what we can be*?

2. How can faith, humility, and hope guide us in our climb toward change?

3. Why is surrender a catalyst that allows a watershed moment to emerge?

Chapter 3: HIDING IN CAVES

Turning Points

1. Why do zealous attempts to completely overhaul ourselves typically end in burnout?

2. Has God ever provided you with a "cave" to rest in while circumstances are difficult? (A cave may look like a trusted friend, a quiet
   place, a passage in the Bible, or a place to retreat.) What kind of
   insight or revelation did your cave arouse?
3. How do pride and entitlement get in the way of godly humility?
4. How can uttering the prayer "Lord, bend me" usher in a watershed
   moment of humility and growth?

Chapter 4: UNRAVELING KNOTS OF DYSFUNCTION

Turning Points

1. If families are God's nests, created so we can grow in and then fly
   from, why are these nests so influential in how we view the world
   and ourselves, even after we've left our nests for good?
2. Dysfunction, favoritism, and generational poor choices can leave our
   lives in knots. Are there any knots you've tried to unravel from the
   rope of your family? Did the knot (or you) unravel in the process?
3. How can acknowledging, accepting, and anticipating new life help
   us to unravel the knots of our past?

Chapter 5: LOVE LIKE A BEE STING

Turning Points

1. How can favoritism in a family be more damaging than neglect?
2. Can the accomplishments of their children take the place of a parent's own affirmation or blessing from God?
3. A manipulative parent invites a child to be openly rebellious or
   quietly passive. How are both of these reactions destructive within
   the dynamics of a family?

Chapter 6: VISIONARIES

Turning Points

1. What is the difference between a dream and a vision?
2. Visionaries are those who dare to put their desire on the line.
   They're willing to take talk and give it legs, to take prayer and help
   it fly. When everyone else is wringing their hands in worry and
   defeat, God wants us to be the ones who take a God-centered vision

and forge ahead. Do you see yourself as a visionary or as someone who merely reacts to the routine of life? If you don't think you're a visionary, what can you do to respond to God's prodding toward this life of vision?

3. The visionary Nehemiah prayed for four months before sharing his vision with anyone. Do you ever feel like prayer is a weak substitute for action? How does Nehemiah's prayer model dispute this misconception?

4. Why do God-centered visions often meet with opposition?

Chapter 7: BRICK BY BRICK

Turning Points

1. Oswald Chambers writes, "God expects His children to be so confident in Him that in any crisis they are the reliable ones." Are you reliable in a crisis or do you succumb to hand-wringing worry?

2. Protective walls in our lives are the unseen barriers designed by God to shelter us, the safeguards that steer us toward good choices and sane options. What happens when compulsion, frailty, and deception contribute to the crumbling of our walls?

3. In an effort to "shoo the foxes" of defeat off the wall he was rebuilding Nehemiah did three things: he acknowledged the damage; he focused on the work, not the threats; and he submitted a strategy to protect the people from an attack. Which of these suggestions can you use to rebuff the negative effects of doubt or frustration regarding a God-centered vision in your life?

Chapter 8: TRYING TO BE KING

Turning Points

1. How can a woman be vulnerable without being perceived to be weak and a pushover, or dominating and controlling?

2. The greatest influence God has designed for a man — after his own relationship with God — is that of a woman. Why do we sometimes feel like adversaries rather than influencers?

3. How does blame become the tool for a woman who likes control and a man who shrinks back in passivity?

Chapter 9: INFLUENCE, NOT CONTROL

Turning Points

1. To influence is to shape and to offer words, advice, prayers, and love for a grander purpose, namely, to bring forth the beauty of God in someone else. How do you influence the lives of the people around you?
2. Influencers know how to build other people's potential rather than thinking they have to take on every challenge themselves. Why are we prone to take on people's problems rather than influence them?
3. Jesus is called the Son of God and the Son of Man, but how is he also the Son of Influence?

Chapter 10: THE PRESSURE TO PLEASE

Turning Points

1. How can pleasing people in a godly way become compromised and reduced to saying yes to avoid disappointment or making people mad?
2. Is your personality more like the apostles Paul or Peter? Which of these two biblical figures seems to be more prone to pleasing?
3. Given a world that promotes personal success, what do you think Oswald Chambers meant when he wrote, "The test of our spiritual life is the power to descend ... The mount is not meant to *teach* us anything, it is meant to *make* us something"?

Chapter 11: LOVE PEOPLE — BUT PLEASE GOD

Turning Points

1. People-Pleasing Thread #1: "Pleasers want things to be smooth, free from turmoil or conflict — no matter the cost." How is this thread impossible to maintain? What are some of the "costs" of maintaining this approval?
2. Thread #2: "Pleasers often sacrifice purpose for performance." Why is performance-based acceptance often the mind-set of a people pleaser?
3. Thread #3: "Pleasers need approval in order to cover a scar or a lonely heart." What kind of wounds do we bandage with excessive people pleasing?

4. Thread #4: "Pleasers often find themselves in a compromising state because they're trying to accommodate several viewpoints." Why is it difficult to accommodate several viewpoints without losing your own?

Chapter 12: WHEN GOOD DANCES WITH EVIL

Turning Points

1. What is your response to things that scare you? Do you tend to ignore them, obsess over them, or hope they will go away?

2. Do you see a difference in *standing up* for God (going to church, wearing a cross, carrying a Bible) and *standing out* (speaking about God's grace and power, refusing to compromise, bearing fruit)? Where do you most often tend to land — standing up or standing out?

3. Settled belief is digging in and saying, "I won't let fear or frustration thwart the good that God can bring from wicked intent." Why is settled belief a watershed moment in our lives — a moment that changes us for good?

Chapter 13: MATURITY'S PRIZE — SURRENDER

Turning Points

1. When Shadrach, Meshach, and Abednego told Nebuchadnezzar that their God was able to deliver them from the furnace, they spoke with brave confidence. But how is their statement that follows an even greater sign of spiritual maturity: "But even if he does not deliver us, we will not serve your gods or worship the image of gold you have set up"?

2. Have you ever witnessed God's boomerang effect — "what was thrown out as evil comes back a miracle"?

3. When Paul wrote "Do not be overcome by evil, but overcome evil with good" (Romans 12:21), he shared an exhortation that has strengthened generations. How do these words offer hope in the midst of confusion?

Chapter 14: GOD-MOVEMENTS

Turning Points

1. A God-movement is evident when circumstances and faith intersect. Have you witnessed this type of movement in your life — a

time when there can be no other explanation than "God is on the move"? Explain.

2. Most God-movements have three things in common: a time of cutting, a time of healing, and a time of conquering. Why do you think cutting and healing come before conquering?

3. A physical circumcision reminds us of the need to be set apart, while a heart circumcision cuts off anything that is keeping us from doing so. Why does God insist that we have a "heart circumcision" in order to be set apart for his purpose?

4. Do you have a personal Gilgal — a place to heal from wounds or excessive pressure? Describe what this is in your life and why it promotes your experience of healing.

Chapter 15: TIME TO CONQUER

Turning Points

1. Why are we apt to cling to an old strategy, outlook, or belief system when God is leading us toward something new?

2. When Joshua asked the Israelites to be silent as they marched around the wall of Jericho, he was wisely taking into account human nature. Do any of the following ring true for you, your friendship circles, your church, or your workplace? Reflect on how you can overcome the one you practice most often.
   - We talk ourselves out of victory.
   - We get distracted and lose intensity.
   - We get caught up in negativity and feed on one another's fears.

3. What are the walls God wants to tear down in your life?

Notes

1. "Top 10 Watershed Moments in History," Listverse, http://listverse. com/2010/08/28/top-10-watershed-moments-in-history/, August 2010 (accessed January 3, 2013).
2. Kent Nerburn, *Make Me an Instrument of Your Peace: Living in the Spirit of the Prayer of St. Francis* (New York: HarperCollins, 1999), 57–62. Reprinted by permission of HarperCollins Publishers.
3. See Malcolm S. Knowles, Elwood F. Holton, and Richard A. Swanson, *The Adult Learner*, 7th ed. (Burlington, Mass.: Butterworth-Heinemann, 2011), 63.
4. "Bend the Church and Save the World," *Spirit of Revival*, vol.18, no.1.
5. Rick Warren, *The Purpose Driven Life* (Grand Rapids: Zondervan, 2002), 32.
6. See "I Didn't Even Want to Be a Cheerleader," *Daily Mail News*, www.dailymail. co.uk/news/article-2098473/Wanda-Holloway-s-daughter-Shanna-breaks-silence-Texas-Cheerleading-murder-plot.html.
7. Oswald Chambers, *My Utmost for His Highest* (Ulrichsville, Ohio: Barbour, 2000), 17.
8. Andy Stanley, *Visioneering* (Colorado Springs: Multnomah, 1999), 17.
9. Ibid., 114.
10. Ibid., 113.
11. "Study note on Nehemiah 1:4," *Life Application Bible* (Wheaton, Ill.: Tyndale House, 1988), 738.
12. Quoted in *Tora! Tora! Tora!* directed by Richard Fleischer; screenplay by Larry Forrester, Hideo Oguni, and Ryuzo Kikushima (Century City, Calif.: 20th Century Fox, 1970).
13. Chambers, *My Utmost for His Highest*, 162.
14. "Study note on Nehemiah 2:17, 18," *Life Application Bible*, 741.
15. Warren, *Purpose Driven Life*, 37, paraphrasing C. S. Lewis, *The Great Divorce* (New York: HarperOne, 2001), 75.
16. John and Stasi Eldredge, *Captivating: Unlocking the Mystery of a Woman's Soul* (Nashville: Nelson, 2005), 50.
17. Ibid., 52.

18. Cited in Jim Davis, "The Tremendous Influence of a Mother," Focus on God .com, http://focusongod.com/Roles02.html (accessed January 9, 2012).

19. Ibid.

20. Dan Allender and Tremper Longman, *Intimate Allies* (Wheaton, Ill.: Tyndale House, 1995), 82.

21. See Sue and Larry Richards, *Every Woman in the Bible* (Nashville: Nelson, 1999), 94.

22. Warren, *Purpose Driven Life*, 29.

23. Chambers, *My Utmost for His Highest*, 199 – 200, gender-neutral language added.

24. "Study note on Matthew 18:1 – 4," *Life Application Bible*, 1367.

25. Immaculée Ilibagiza, *Left to Tell* (Carlsbad, Calif.: Hay House, 2006), 77.

26. Quoted in "About Us: The Story," Musana Community Development Organization, http://musana.org/AboutUs_TheStory (accessed January 11, 2013).

27. Warren, *Purpose Driven Life*, 203.

28. "Study note on Daniel 3:15," *Life Application Bible*, 1196.

29. "Study note on Joshua 5:2, 3," *Life Application Bible*, 315.

30. Robert Morgan, *On This Day in Christian History* (Nashville: Nelson, 1997), October 8.

31. Ibid.

32. See study note on Joshua 5:10, *Life Application Bible*, 315.

33. Chambers, *My Utmost for His Highest*, 117.

34. Diane Hampton, *The Diet Alternative*, rev. ed. (New Kensington, Pa.: Whitaker House, 2001), 11.

35. Jackie Kendall, *Free Yourself to Forgive* (New York: Hachette, 2009), 54.

36. Mark Batterson, *In a Pit with a Lion on a Snowy Day* (Colorado Springs: Multnomah, 2006), 114.